AKHYAYIKAS

AKHYAYIKAS

100 Short Stories And Anecdotes That Inspire, Coach, Teach and Motivate.

RAJESH SESHADRI

notionpress.com

INDIA • SINGAPORE • MALAYSIA

ISBN 979-8-88849-051-8

This book is dedicated to all story-tellers, known and unknown, who have significantly impacted human thought and behaviour. The beauty of stories is that they move, teach, ignite, inspire and motivate without appearing to do so. Lecturing and preaching may have little impact on teenagers and young adults, least with mature adults; but stories have an inexorable way of getting the message across.

This is a work of fiction. Names, characters, businesses, places, events and incidents are either the products of imagination or used in a fictitious manner. Any resemblance to actual persons, living or dead, or actual events is purely coincidental.

I claim no ownership over the stories themselves, which originate from tales I have heard or been told throughout my life; they belong solely to their narrators, authors, writers or creators, which for the purpose of this book are either unknown or unavailable; the stories themselves have however been edited, improvised upon and embellished where necessary. I shall endeavour to systematically edit this book to include sources where I can and remove any story that may unintentionally have been infringing on any copyright.

Although I have made every possible effort to ensure that the information in this book was correct at publishing time, I do not assume and hereby disclaim any liability to any party for any loss, damage, or disruption caused by errors or omissions, whether such errors or omissions result from negligence, accident, or any other cause.

CONTENTS

CONTENTS

CONTENTS

CONTENTS

CONTENTS

About the Author

In addition to being a seasoned corporate professional who has risen from the grassroots to C-suite levels in a career spanning almost three decades, Rajesh Seshadri continues to don multiple hats – that of a coach, mentor, trainer, and therapist. His LinkedIn profile (https://in.linkedin.com/in/rajeshseshadri) encapsulates his corporate career.

He is a Fellow Member of the ICAI – FCMA in addition to having a dual PGD in Finance & Human Resource Management. His enthusiasm to help people discover and unleash their potential, grow and develop led him to learn various psychological tools including clinical hypnotherapy, Gestalt and Silva Ultra. He is a certified Leadership Coach and certified Life Coach and a member of various bodies and associations, including the APA, AAH, ISTD, AIMA and BMA.

He is married to Prema and they have a teenage son, Prakrut and they live in Mumbai.

The author has often relied on stories in coaching, training, and therapy and has found it immensely invaluable, even to the extent of using metaphor in corporate meetings and discussions. This is primarily due to the fact that the 'listener' does not respond to the story as an 'opinion' or 'advice'.

He says, *"So often, I can feel the energy shift in the room as people take in the impact of what a simple poignant story can express. No amount of lectures, power points or vision and mission statements can so pithily and impressively convey what a story can."*

Do you have a story you would like to share?

Write in to me@rajeshseshadri.com or visit
www.rajeshseshadri.com

*"The human species thinks in metaphors
and learns through stories."*
– Mary Catherine Bateson

Preface

Metaphorical thinking is fundamental to cognition, communication and our 'narrative mind'. This makes it a valuable tool for helping friends, family, colleagues and clients gain new perspectives on their lives. Using a metaphor is a helpful way of talking about emotional and relational experience.

The mind has the capacity to understand new ideas by relating them to concepts it is familiar with. Using metaphor has been a tradition in all the major schools of therapy and is a particularly helpful way of talking about emotional and relational experience.

I often rely on stories in coaching, training, workshops and therapy and have found it immensely invaluable. This is due to the fact that the "listener" does not respond to the story as an "opinion" or "advice" from me. Neither does the image he has of me as a person / individual filter the content or create a barrier in the way his mind would digest and assimilate the narrative.

So often, I can feel the energy shift in the room as people take in the impact of what a simple poignant story can express. No amount of lectures, power points or vision and mission statements can so pithily and impressively convey what a story can.

Whether you acknowledge it or not, each little story in this book will leave an imprint on your mind, as it has done on mine. I can honestly and gratefully attribute several learnings in my life span to stories.

INTRODUCTION

If I told you that this book was written especially for you, you would perhaps laugh it off. You would find it incredulous. Yet, right now, of all the places you could have been and of all the things you could be doing, you have purchased or downloaded and are reading this book. Or perhaps it was gifted to you by a friend and you decided to go ahead and see what the book is all about.

I am happy you are reading this book and for the changes that will definitely occur. Whether you believe it or not, every story in this book will leave an imprint on your mind. I take the liberty of stating further it is neither an accident nor a coincidence.

The Universe have a funny way of bringing us to the exact people, places, circumstances, and messages that our souls are calling for at the right time. This phenomenon of apparently meaningful coincidences is what Dr. Deepak Chopra calls *synchronicity*.

Yet, this is not a novel! So reading it the way you read novels would be near impossible. Feel free to jump to any page at random and the particular story you happen to read will make perfect sense to you in terms of timing and meaning! Let me know if it doesn't!

I won't keep you from the stories any longer. May this book bring you newfound understanding, joy, hope, peace, learning, illumination or anything that you wish for.

"A lost coin is found by means of a candle;
the deepest truth is found by means
of a simple story."
– Anthony De Mello

CHAPTER ONE

BE THE BOSS

A horse suddenly came galloping swiftly down the road. It seemed as though the man had somewhere important to go.

Another man, who was standing alongside the road, shouted, "Where are you going?" and the man on the horse replied, "I don't know! Ask the horse!"

This short, well known Zen story has a powerful teaching behind it. The horse is symbolic of our habitual energy, or what drives us on auto-pilot most times. This story tells us the funny way we usually live: at the mercy of our habits that haven't come from intentional actions, but rather mindless activity and surroundings instead.

Our habitual energy drags us along, pulling us in every direction at a hurried pace and we don't even know why. Stop to ask yourself why you are running around so much and you might be surprised at the lack of answers coming forth. And when you do find an answer, it's usually not a great one. You've become used to it because that is how we were taught to live.

Forget the running around aimlessly, it gets us nowhere. Learn how to take the reins and let the horse know who is the boss.

CHAPTER TWO

Judge Not

Once upon the time there was an old farmer who had worked his crops for many years.

One day his horse ran away. Upon hearing the news, his neighbours came to visit. "Such bad luck," they said sympathetically.

"Maybe," the farmer replied.

The next morning the horse returned, bringing with it three other wild horses. "How wonderful," the neighbors exclaimed.

"Maybe," replied the old man.

The following day, his son tried to ride one of the untamed horses, was thrown, and broke his leg. The neighbors again came to offer their sympathy on his misfortune.

"Maybe," answered the farmer.

The day after, military officials came to the village to draft young men into the army. Seeing that the son's leg was broken, they passed him by. The neighbors congratulated the farmer on how well things had turned out.

"Maybe," said the farmer.

No event can be judged in a conclusive manner. Our lives aren't fictional plays with "Acts" and "Stages" - there aren't absolute breaks which separate one moment from another, and there isn't one final formula which everything leads up to.

CHAPTER THREE

You First

There was once a pair of acrobats. The teacher was a poor widower and the student was a young girl by the name of Mili. These acrobats performed each day on the streets in order to earn enough to eat.

Their act consisted of the teacher balancing a tall bamboo pole on his head while the little girl climbed slowly to the top. Once to the top, she remained there while the teacher walked along the ground.

Both performers had to maintain complete focus and balance in order to prevent any injury from occurring and to complete the performance. One day, the teacher said to the pupil: "Listen Mili, I will watch you and you watch me, so that we can help each other maintain concentration and balance and prevent an accident. Then we'll surely earn enough to eat."

But the little girl was wise, she answered, "Dear master, I think it would be better for each of us to watch ourselves. To look after oneself means to look after both of us. That way I am sure we will avoid any accidents and earn enough to eat."

This story was said to have been taught by the Buddha himself. It is meant to show that taking care of yourself is imperative to take care of others. We must help ourselves in order to help anyone else.

CHAPTER FOUR

THE EMPTY BOX

The story goes that some time ago, a man punished his 3-year-old daughter for wasting a roll of gold wrapping paper. Money was tight and he became infuriated when the child tried to decorate a box to put under the Christmas tree.

Nevertheless, the little girl brought the gift to her father the next morning and said, "This is for you, Daddy."

He was embarrassed by his earlier overreaction, but his anger flared again when he found the box was empty.

He yelled at her, "Don't you know that when you give someone a present, there's supposed to be something inside it?"

The little girl looked up at him with tears in her eyes and said, "Oh, Daddy, it is not empty. I blew kisses into the box. All for you, Daddy."

The father was crushed. He put his arms around his little girl, and he begged for her forgiveness.

Is there anything more precious than unconditional love?

"The ultimate lesson all of us have to learn is unconditional love, which includes not only others but ourselves as well.

Elisabeth Kubler-Ross

CHAPTER FIVE

A Glass of Milk

One day, a poor boy who was selling goods from door to door to pay his way through school, found he had only one thin dime left, and he was hungry. He decided he would ask for a meal at the next house. However, he lost his nerve when a lovely young woman opened the door. Instead of a meal he asked for a drink of water.

She thought he looked hungry so brought him a large glass of milk. He drank it slowly, and then asked, "How much do I owe you?"

"You don't owe me anything," she replied. "Mother has taught us never to accept pay for a kindness."

He said, "Then I thank you from my heart." As Howard Kelly left that house, he not only felt stronger physically, but his faith in God and man was strong also. He had been ready to give up and quit.

Many years later that young woman became critically ill. The local doctors were baffled. They finally sent her to the big city, where they called in specialists to study her rare disease. Dr. Howard Kelly was called in for the consultation. When he heard the name of the town she came from, a strange light filled his eyes. Immediately he rose and went down the hall of the hospital to her room.

Dressed in his doctor's gown he went in to see her. He recognized her at once. He went back to the consultation room determined to do his best to save her life. From that day he gave special attention to the case.

After a long struggle, the battle was won. Dr. Kelly requested the business office to pass the final bill to him for approval.

He looked at it, then wrote something on the edge and the bill was sent to her room. She feared to open it, for she was sure it would take the rest of her life to pay for it all. Finally she looked, and something caught her attention on the side of the bill.

She read these words.....

Paid in full with one glass of milk.

(Signed)

Dr. Howard Kelly

"No act of kindness, no matter how small, is ever wasted.

Aesop

CHAPTER SIX

THE ONE-EYED MOTHER

Vincent's mom had only one eye.

Vincent hated it because she was such an embarrassment. She cooked for students and teachers to support the family.

There was this one day when he was in primary school and a Parent-Teacher meet was organized. He was so embarrassed that he ignored her, threw her a hateful look and ran out.

The next day at school, several of his classmates and many others pointed out to him, "Hey - your mom only has one eye!"

He wanted to bury himself. He wished his mom would just disappear.

He confronted her that day and said, "Could you stop making me a laughing stock amongst people?"

His mom did not respond, but she did ensure that she never came to visit him in school again.

Vincent was so full of anger that he was oblivious of her feelings, he didn't even ponder or spare a second thought to what he had said. He wanted to have nothing to do with her, he just wanted to go out of that house so he studied real hard, got a scholarship and went abroad to study.

Over time, he got married, bought a house of his own and was a proud father of two kids. One day, his Mother paid them a surprise visit. She hadn't seen him for many years and she had never met his grandchildren – she was so eager to meet his grandchildren.

When she stood by the door, his children stared at her in horror, and Vincent yelled at her for coming over uninvited. "How dare you come to my house and scare my children! Get out of here – NOW!"

His mother quietly answered, "Oh, I'm so sorry. I may have gotten the wrong address."

One day, a letter regarding an old school reunion came to Vincent's house. After the reunion, he went to the old shack just out of curiosity.

His neighbors told him that she had passed away – Vincent did not shed a single tear. They handed him a letter that she had wanted him to have, in case he ever visited.

"My dearest and only son,

I think of you all the time. I'm sorry that I came to your house and scared your children. I was so glad when I heard you were coming for the reunion. But I may not be able to even get out of bed to see you. I'm sorry that I was a constant embarrassment to you when you were growing up.

You see when you were very little, you got into an accident, slipped into a coma, and lost your eye. As a mother, I couldn't stand watching you having to grow up with one eye. So I gave you mine. I was so proud of my son who was seeing a whole new world for me, in my place, with that eye.

With all my love to you,
Your mother."

CHAPTER SEVEN

TAKING IT FOR GRANTED

That evening, Brij quarrelled with his mom and then stormed out of the house.

On the way, he remembered that he did not have any money in his pocket; in fact he did not even have enough coins to make a phone call home.

At that time, he happened to pass by a street hawker, who amongst other things, was selling noodles. The fragrance wafted through the air and suddenly, he felt very hungry.

The seller saw him hesitating and faltering even as he was eyeing what was on offer.

He asked, "Hey young lad, you want to eat a bowl of noodles?"

Brij replied, a touch of remorse in his speech, "I have no money, I ran away from my home but forgot to take what little I had saved. In fact, I have no money to make a call to my home either, I don't know what to do."

The seller looked at him kindly, "Here, I will cook you a bowl."

As Brij scooped the first batch noodles into his mouth with relish, tears streamed from eyes.

"What happened?" asked the seller.

"Nothing. I am just touched by your kindness", Brij said as he wiped away the tears.

The seller sighed and said, "Young lad, I am surprised how you think. Think again. I only gave you a bowl of noodles and you felt that way. Your mother had raised you since you were born, what happened to your sense of gratitude then?"

"Why did I not think of that? A bowl of noodles from a stranger made me feel indebted, and my mother has raised me from birth and I have never felt grateful. I think I have taken her for granted."

The seller lent him a few coins to take a bus home and Brij rushed into his mother's arms, forever indebted.

"Sometimes, we should express our gratitude for the small and simple things like the scent of the rain, the taste of your favourite food, or the sound of a loved one's voice.

Joseph B. Wirthlin

CHAPTER EIGHT

MUDA

The prestigious hotel group had invited Mr. Masai Imai from Japan to hold a workshop for its staff.

The staff were very sceptical - the hotel is doing excellent business, this person from Japan has no exposure to hotel industry - what exactly is he going to teach?

But everybody gathered as planned for the workshop in the conference hall sharp at 9 am.

Mr. Masai was introduced to them - a not so impressive personality, nor the English all that good; spoke as if he was first formulating each sentence in Japanese and then translating it into rather clumsy English.

"Good morning! Let's start work. I am told this is a workshop; but I see neither work nor shop. So let's proceed where work is happening Let's start with the first room on the first floor."

Mr. Masai, followed by the senior management, the participants, the video camera crew trouped out of the conference room and proceeded to the destination.

That happened to be the laundry room of the hotel. Mr. Masai entered the room and stood at the window, "Beautiful view!" he said.

The staff knew it; they need not invite a Japanese consultant to tell them this!

"A room with such a beautiful view is being wasted as a laundry room. Shift the laundry to the basement and convert this into a guest room."

Aha! Now nobody had ever thought about that!

The manager said, "Yes, it can be done."

"Then let's do it," Mr. Masai said.

"Yes sir, I will make a note of this and we will include it in the report on the workshop that will be prepared." Said the Manager

"Excuse me, but there is nothing to note down in this. Let's just do it, right now." Mr. Masai.

"Right now?"

"Yes, decide on a room on the ground floor/basement and shift the stuff out of this room right away. It should take a couple of hours, right?" asked Mr. Masai.

"Yes." Said the Manager.

"Let's come back here just before lunch. By then all this stuff will have got shifted out and the room must be ready with the carpets, furniture etc. and from today you can start earning the few thousand that you charge your customers for a night."

"Ok, Sir." The manager had no option.

The next destination was the pantry. The group entered. At the entrance were two huge sinks full of plates to be washed.

Mr. Masai removed his jacket and started washing the plates.

"Sir, Please, what are you doing?" the manager didn't know what to say and what to do.

"Why, I am washing the plates", Mr. Masai.

"But sir, there is staff here to do that." Mr. Masai continued washing, "I think sink is for washing plates, there are stands here to keep the plates and the plates should go into the stands."

All the officials wondered - did they require a consultant to tell them this?

After finishing the job, Mr. Masai asked, "How many plates do you have?'

"Plenty, so that there should never be any shortage." answered the Manager.

Mr. Masai said, "We have a word in Japanese - 'Muda'. Muda means delay, Muda means unnecessary spending. One lesson to be learned in this workshop is to avoid both. If you have plenty of plates, there will be delay in cleaning them up. The first step to correct this situation is to remove all the excess plates."

"Yes, we will say this in the report." Manager.

"No, wasting our time in writing the report is again an instance of 'Muda'. We must pack the extra plates in a box right away and send these to whichever other section of Taj requires these. Throughout the workshop now we will find out where all we find this 'Muda' hidden."

And then at every spot and session, the staff eagerly awaited to find out Muda and learn how to avoid it.

On the last day, Mr. Masai told a story.

"A Japanese and an American, both fond of hunting, met in a jungle. They entered deep jungle and suddenly realized that they had run out of bullets. Just then they heard a lion roaring. Both started running. But the Japanese took a short break to put on his sports shoes.

The American said, "What are you doing? We must first get to the car."

The Japanese responded, "No. I only have to ensure that I remain ahead of you."

All the participants engrossed in listening to the story, realized suddenly that the lion would stop after getting his victim!

"The lesson is: competition in today's world is so fierce, that it is important to stay ahead of other, even by just a couple of steps. And you have such a huge and naturally well-endowed country. If you remember to curtail your production expenditure and give the best quality always, you will be miles ahead as compared to so many other countries in the world.", concluded Mr. Masai.

It is never late to learn – let us take the MUDA out of our lives!

"Efficiency is doing things right, Effectiveness is doing the right things.

Peter Drucker

CHAPTER NINE

Leaving a Good Taste

There was an old man who was admitted in a hospital.

A young man was visiting him every day, and sits with him for more than one hour. He helps him eat his food, and to take his shower.

Then he takes him walking in the garden of the hospital. After that he brings him back to his room and helps him to lie down.

He goes away after reassuring himself that the old man is doing well.

One day the nurse entered his room, to give him medicine and inspect his condition, and said to him: "May the Lord be always gracious to your kind and caring son. Every day he visits you and shows great care."

The old man looked at her and closed his eyes and said to her: "I wish it was one of my children. This is an orphan from the neighbourhood where we live. I met him one day in the past, crying at the door of a Temple, after his father died. I comforted him and bought for him candy.

I neither saw him nor talked to him for a very long time. When he grew up and came to discover where my wife and I were living. He was visiting us every day to inspect our conditions. When I later fell sick, he took my old wife to his home. He then comes to the hospital to see my treatment every day.

One day I asked him: "My son why do you have to deal with us and care about us?"

He simply smiled and then said: "The taste of the candy is still in my mouth."

CHAPTER TEN

HERITAGE

At the point of death, Tom Smith called his children and he advised them to follow his footsteps so that they can have peace of mind in all that they do.

His daughter, Sara, said, "Daddy, it is unfortunate you are dying without a penny in your bank. Other fathers that you tag as being greedy, corrupt, thieves of public funds left houses and properties for their children; even this house we live in is a rented apartment. Sorry, I can't emulate you, just go, let's chart our own course.

Few moments later, their father gave up the spirit.

Three years later, Sara went for an interview in a multinational company.

At interview the Chairman of the committee asked, "Which Smith are you?"

Sara replied, "I am Sara Smith. My Dad Tom Smith is now late....."

Chairman cuts in, "O my God, you are Tom Smith's daughter?"

He turned to the other members and said, "This Smith man was the one that signed my membership form into the Institute of Administrators and his recommendation earned me where I am today. He did all these free. I didn't even know his address, he never knew me. He just did it for me."

He turned to Sara, "I have no questions for you, consider yourself as having gotten this job, come tomorrow, your letter will be waiting for you."

Sara Smith became the Corporate Affairs Manager of the company with two Cars with Drivers, A duplex attached to the office, and a salary of £1,000,000 per month excluding allowances and other costs.

After two years of working in the company, the MD of the company came from America to announce his intention to resign and needed a replacement. A personality with high integrity was sought after, again the company's consultant nominated Sara Smith.

In an interview, she was asked the secret of her success.

With tears, she replied, "My daddy paved these ways for me. It was after he died that I knew that he was financially poor but immensely rich in integrity, discipline and honesty".

She was asked again, why she is weeping since she is no longer a kid as to miss her dad still after a long time.

She replied, "At the point of death, I insulted my dad for being an honest man of integrity. I hope he will forgive me in his grave now. I didn't work for all these, he did it for me to just walk in".

So, finally she was asked, "Will you follow your father's footsteps as he requested ?"

And her simple answer was, "1 now adore the man, I have a big picture of him in my living room and at the entrance of my house. He deserves whatever I have after God".

Leave a good heritage for your children

CHAPTER ELEVEN

THE GUIDEPOST

The son didn't like living in his father's house. This was because of his father's constant 'nagging' -

"You are leaving the room without switching off the fan"

"The TV is on in the room where there is no one. Switch it off!"

"Keep the pen in the stand; it is fallen down"

The son didn't like his father nagging him for these minor things. He had to tolerate these things till yesterday since he was with them in the same house.

But today, however, he had an invitation for a job interview. "As soon as I get the job, I should leave this town. There won't be any nagging from my father" were his thoughts.

As he was about to leave for the interview, the father advised: "Answer the questions put to you without any hesitation. Even if you don't know the answer, mention that confidently." His gave him more money than he actually needed to attend the interview.

The son arrived at the interview centre. He noticed that there were no security guards at the gate. Even though the door was open, the latch was protruding out probably hitting the people entering through the door. He put the latch back properly, closed the door and entered the office.

On both sides of the pathway he could see beautiful flower plants. The gardener had kept the water running in the hose-pipe and was not to be seen anywhere. The water was overflowing on the pathway. He lifted the hosepipe and placed it near one of the plants and went further.

There was no one in the reception area. However, there was a notice saying that the interview was on the first floor. He slowly climbed the stairs.

The light that was switched on last night was still burning at 10 am in the morning. He remembered his father's admonition, "Why are you leaving the room without switching off the light?" and thought he could still hear that now. Even though he felt irritated by that thought, he sought the switch and switched off the light.

Upstairs in a large hall he could see many aspirants sitting waiting for their turn. He looked at the number of people and wondered if he had any chance of getting the job.

He entered the hall with some trepidation and stepped on the *Welcome* mat placed near the door. He noticed that the mat was upside down. He straightened out the mat with some irritation. Habits die hard.

He saw that in a few rows in the front there were many people waiting for their turn, whereas the back rows were empty, but a number of fans were running over those rows of seats.

He heard his father's voice again, "Why are the fans running in the room where there is no one?" He switched off the fans that were not needed and sat at one of the empty chairs. He could see many men entering the interview room and immediately leave from another door.

There was thus no way anyone could guess what was being asked in the interview.

When it was his turn, He went and stood before the interviewer with some trepidation and concern.

The officer took the certificates from him and without looking at them asked, "When can you start work?"

He thought, "is this a trick question being asked in the interview, or is this a signal that I have been offered the job?" He was confused.

"What are you thinking?" asked the boss. "We didn't ask anyone any question here. By asking a few questions we won't be able to assess the skills of anyone. So our test was to assess the attitude of the person. We kept certain tests based on the behaviour of the candidates and we observed everyone through CCTV."

"No one who came today did anything to set right the latch at the door, the hose pipe, the welcome mat, the uselessly running fans or lights. You were the only one who did that. That's why we have decided to select you for the job", said the boss.

He always used to get irritated at his father's discipline and demonstrations. Now he realized that it is only the discipline that has got him his job. His irritation and anger at his father vanished completely.

For us to become a beautiful sculpture and a human being we need to accept admonitions that chisel out the bad habits and behaviour from ourselves. That is what our father does when he disciplines us.

The mother lifts the child up on her waist to feed her, to cuddle her, and to put her to sleep. But the father is not like that. He lifts the child up on his shoulders to make her see the world that he couldn't see.

Our father is our teacher when we are five years old; a terrible villain when we are about twenty, and a guidepost as long as he lives.

Are you a guidepost?

CHAPTER TWELVE

THE MEANING OF SILENCE

Four Monks Decided to Meditate Silently without speaking for two weeks.

They began with enthusiasm and no one said a word the whole day. By nightfall of the first day, the candle began to flicker and then went out.

The First Monk blurted out, "Oh, No! The candle is out!"

The Second Monk said, "Hey! We are not supposed to speak!"

The Third Monk said in an irritated voice, "What is this? Why did you two break the Silence?"

The Fourth Monk smiled and said, "Wow! I'm the only one who hasn't spoken."

The reason why each monk broke the silence, is a common stumbling block in our inner journey.

Distraction led the first monk to forget the practice of witnessing without reacting. Judgement led the second to forget he was guilty himself. Emotional Intelligence (anger) did the third one in. Pride made the fourth lose his way.

Reward is in the effort, not in the recognition.
It is the privilege of knowledge to speak; it is the privilege of Wisdom to Listen.

CHAPTER THIRTEEN

UNEVEN DUCKS

A father left 17 ducks as asset for his three Sons. When their father passed away, his sons opened up the will. The Will of their father stated that the eldest son should get half of 17 ducks, the middle son should be given $1/3^{rd}$ of 17 ducks, and that the youngest son should be given $1/9^{th}$ of the 17 ducks.

As it is not possible to divide 17 into half or 17 by 3 or 17 by 9, the sons started to fight with each other. So, they decided to go to a wise man who lived in a cave.

The wise man listened patiently about the Will. The wise man, after giving this thought, brought one duck of his own & added the same to 17. That increased the total to 18 ducks.

Now, he started reading the deceased father's will.

Half of 18 = 9. So he gave 9 ducks to the eldest son.

$1/3^{rd}$ of 18 = 6. So he gave 6 ducks to the middle son.

$1/9^{th}$ of 18 = 2. So he gave 2 ducks to the youngest son.

Now add this up: 9 + 6 + 2 = 17 and this leaves 1 duck which the wise man took back.

The attitude of negotiation & problem solving is to find the 18th duck i.e. the common ground. Once a person is able to find the common ground, the issue is resolved.

CHAPTER FOURTEEN

PUT THE GLASS DOWN!

A psychologist walked around a room while teaching stress management to an audience. As she raised a glass of water, everyone expected they'd be asked the "half empty or half full" question. Instead, with a smile on her face, she inquired: "How heavy is this glass of water?"

Answers called out ranged from 200 gms to 500 gms.

She replied, "The absolute weight doesn't matter. It depends on how long I hold it. If I hold it for a minute, it's not a problem. If I hold it for an hour, I'll have an ache in my arm. If I hold it for a day, my arm will feel numb and paralyzed. In each case, the weight of the glass doesn't change, but the longer I hold it, the heavier it becomes."

She continued, "The stresses and worries in life are like that glass of water. Think about them for a while and nothing happens. Think about them a bit longer and they begin to hurt. And if you think about them all day long, you will feel paralyzed – incapable of doing anything."

It's important to remember to let go of your stresses. As early in the evening as you can, put all your burdens down. Don't carry them through the evening and into the night. Remember to put the glass down!

"Stress is nothing more than a socially acceptable form of mental illness.

Richard Carlson

CHAPTER FIFTEEN

No Witnesses

Once Ramakrishna Paramhansa asked the disciples of his ashram to steal a little rice from their own home with a condition that nobody sees them stealing.

Next day almost everyone proudly came with rice in the ashram as they had completed the task assigned to them by the Guru,

Yet, Swami Vivekananda came empty handed.

On being asked the reason, he told that how much ever he tried, he always saw himself stealing the rice.

He couldn't do because however harder he tried to hide his deeds from the world, he knew his self is witnessing it.

So there never exists a situation when you can hide your deeds from everyone, because you know what you are doing and it can be never hidden from your SELF.

Ramakrishna Paramhansa knew that Vivekananda's honesty and innocence will make him his chief disciple one day.

CHAPTER SIXTEEN

THE COMPLICATION

A cruise ship met with an accident at sea, on the ship was a pair of couple. After having made their way to the lifeboat, they realized that there was space for only one person.

At this moment the man pushed the woman behind him and jumped onto the lifeboat himself. The lady stood on the sinking ship and shouted one sentence to her husband.

Teacher: "What do you think she shouted?"

Most of the students excitedly answered, "I hate you! I was blind!"

Now, the teacher noticed a boy who was silent throughout, she got him to answer.

Boy: "Teacher, I believe she would have shouted - Take care of our child!"

Teacher (with surprise): "Have you heard this story before?"

Boy: "Nope, but that was what my mum told my dad before she died to disease".

The teacher lamented, "The answer is right".

The cruise sunk, the man went home and brought up their daughter single-handedly. Many years later after the death of the man, their daughter found his diary while tidying his belongings. It turns out that when parents went onto the cruise ship, the mother was already diagnosed with a terminal illness. At the critical moment, the father rushed to the only chance of survival.

He wrote in his diary, "How I wished to sink to the bottom of the ocean with you, but for the sake of our daughter, I can only let you lie forever below the sea alone".

The class was silent.

CHAPTER SEVENTEEN

TRUTH IS DECEPTIVE

A 24 year old boy seeing out from the train's window shouted, "Dad, look the trees are going behind!"

Dad smiled and a young couple sitting nearby, looked at the 24 year old's childish behaviour with pity, suddenly he again exclaimed -

"Dad, look the clouds are running with us!"

The couple couldn't resist and said to the old man, "Why don't you take your son to a good doctor?"

The old man smiled and said, "I did and we are just coming from the hospital, my son was blind from birth, he just got his eyes today."

"We should not pretend to understand the world only by our intellect. The judgement of the intellect is only part of the truth.

Carl Jung

CHAPTER EIGHTEEN

THE CONTAINER AND CONTENTS

A group of alumni, highly established in their careers, got together to visit their old university professor. Conversation soon turned into complaints about stress at work and in life. Offering his guests coffee, the professor went to the kitchen and returned with a large pot of coffee and an assortment of cups - porcelain, plastic, glass, crystal, some plain looking, some expensive, some exquisite - telling them to help themselves to the coffee.

When all the students had a cup of coffee in hand, the professor said: "If you noticed, all the nice looking expensive cups have been taken up, leaving behind the plain and cheap ones. While it is normal for you to want only the best for yourselves, that is the source of your problems and stress. Be assured that the cup itself adds no quality to the coffee."

"In most cases it is just more expensive and in some cases even hides what we drink. What all of you really wanted was coffee, not the cup, but you consciously went for the best cups! And then you began eyeing each other's cups."

"Now consider this: Life is the coffee; the jobs, money and position in society are the cups. They are just tools to hold and contain Life, and the type of cup we have does not define, nor change the quality of life we live. Sometimes, by concentrating only on the cup, we fail to enjoy the coffee. Savour the coffee, not the cups!"

CHAPTER NINETEEN

WHAT GOES AROUND

One day a man saw an old lady, stranded on the side of the road, but even in the dim light of day, he could see she needed help. So he pulled up in front of her Mercedes and got out. His Pontiac was still sputtering when he approached her.

Even with the smile on his face, she looked worried. No one had stopped to help for the last hour or so. Was he going to hurt her? He didn't look safe; he looked poor and hungry.

He could see that she was frightened, standing out there in the cold. He knew how she felt. It was those chills which only fear can put in you.

He said, 'I'm here to help you, ma'am. Why don't you wait in the car where it's warm? By the way, my name is Bryan Anderson.'

Well, all she had was a flat tire, but for an old lady, that was bad enough. Bryan crawled under the car looking for a place to put the jack, skinning his knuckles a time or two.

Soon he was able to change the tire. But he had to get dirty and his hands hurt.

As he was tightening up the lug nuts, she rolled down the window and began to talk to him. She told him that she was from St. Louis and was only just passing through. She couldn't thank him enough for coming to her aid.

Bryan just smiled as he closed her trunk. The lady asked how much she owed him. Any amount would have been all right with her. She already imagined all the awful things that could have happened had he not stopped. Bryan never thought twice about being paid.

This was not a job to him. This was helping someone in need, and God knows there were plenty, who had given him a hand in the past. He had lived his whole life that way, and it never occurred to him to act any other way.

He told her that if she really wanted to pay him back, the next time she saw someone who needed help, she could give that person the assistance they needed, and Bryan added, 'And think of me.'

He waited until she started her car and drove off. It had been a cold and depressing day, but he felt good as he headed for home, disappearing into the twilight.

A few miles down the road the lady saw a small cafe. She went in to grab a bite to eat, and take the chill off before she made the last leg of her trip home. It was a dingy looking restaurant. Outside were two old gas pumps. The whole scene was unfamiliar to her. The waitress came over and brought a clean towel to wipe her wet hair. She had a sweet smile, one that even being on her feet for the whole day couldn't erase. The lady noticed the waitress was nearly eight months pregnant, but she never let the strain and aches change her attitude. The old lady wondered how someone who had so little could be so giving to a stranger. Then she remembered Bryan...

After the lady finished her meal, she paid with a hundred dollar bill. The waitress quickly went to get change for her hundred dollar bill, but the old lady had slipped right out the door. She was gone by the time the waitress came back. The waitress wondered where the lady could be. Then she noticed something written on the napkin.

There were tears in her eyes when she read what the lady wrote: 'You don't owe me anything. I have been there too. Somebody once helped me out, the way I'm helping you. If you really want to pay me back, here is what you do: Do not let this chain of love end with you.'

Under the napkin were four more $100 bills.

Well, there were tables to clear, sugar bowls to fill, and people to serve, but the waitress made it through another day. That night when she got home from work and climbed into bed, she was thinking about the money and what the lady had written. How could the lady have known how much she and her husband needed it? With the baby due next month, it was going to be hard.

She knew how worried her husband was, and as he lay sleeping next to her, she gave him a soft kiss and whispered soft and low, 'Everything's going to be all right. I love you, Bryan Anderson.'

There is an old saying - 'What goes around comes around.'
"Problems or successes, they are all the results of our own actions. Karma. The philosophy of action is that no one else is the giver of peace or happiness. One's own karma, one's own actions are responsible to bring either happiness or success or whatever.

Maharishi Mahesh Yogi

CHAPTER TWENTY

STRUGGLE

A man found the cocoon of a butterfly. One day a small opening appeared. He sat and watched the butterfly for several hours as it struggled to force its body through that little hole. Then it seemed to stop making any progress.

It appeared as if it had gotten as far as it could and could go no further. So the man decided to help the butterfly.

He took a pair of scissors and snipped off the remaining bit of the cocoon. The butterfly then emerged easily. But it had a swollen body and small, shrivelled wings.

The man continued to watch the butterfly because he expected that, at any moment, the wings would enlarge and expand to be able to support the body, which would contract in time. Neither happened!

In fact, the butterfly spent the rest of its life crawling around with a swollen body and shrivelled wings. It never was able to fly. What the man in his kindness and haste did not understand was that the restricting cocoon and the struggle required for the butterfly to get through the tiny opening were nature's way of forcing fluid from the body of the butterfly into its wings so that it would be ready for flight once it achieved its freedom from the cocoon.

Do not oversimplify life for your children, do not smother them with luxury and comforts, they grow stronger with the challenges they have to face in life.

CHAPTER TWENTY-ONE

THROUGH THE LOOKING GLASS

A young couple moved into a new neighbourhood. The next morning while they were eating breakfast, the young woman sees her neighbour hanging the wash outside.

"That laundry is not very clean", she said. "She doesn't know how to wash correctly. Perhaps she needs better laundry soap."

Her husband looked on, but remained silent. Every time her neighbour would hang her wash to dry, the young woman would make the same comment.

About one month later, the woman was surprised to see a nice clean wash on the line and said to her husband: "Look, she has learned how to wash correctly. I wonder who taught her this."

The husband said, "I got up early this morning and cleaned our windows."

CHAPTER TWENTY-TWO

THINKING ON YOUR FEET

An old German shepherd dog starts chasing rabbits and before long, discovers that he's lost. Wandering about, he notices a panther heading rapidly in his direction with the intention of having lunch.

The old German shepherd thinks, "Uh, oh! I'm in deep trouble now!"

Noticing some bones on the ground close by, he immediately settles down to chew on the bones with his back to the approaching cat. Just as the panther is about to leap, the old German shepherd exclaims loudly, "Boy, that was one delicious panther! I wonder, if there are any more around here?"

Hearing this, the young panther halts his attack in mid-strike, a look of terror comes over him and he slinks away into the trees.

"Whew!" says the panther, "That was close! That old German Shepherd nearly had me!"

Meanwhile, a squirrel who had been watching the whole scene from a nearby tree, figures he can put this knowledge to good use and trade it for protection from the panther. So, off he goes.

The squirrel soon catches up with the panther, spills the beans and strikes a deal for himself with the panther.

The young panther is furious at being made a fool of and says, "Here, squirrel, hop on my back and see what's going to happen to that conniving canine!"

Now, the old German Shepherd sees the panther coming with the squirrel on his back and thinks, "What am I going to do now?," but instead of running, the dog sits down with his back to his attackers, pretending he hasn't seen them yet, and just when they get close enough to hear, the old German Shepherd says...

"Where's that squirrel? I sent him off an hour ago to bring me another panther!"

"It is by presence of mind in untried emergencies that the native mettle of man is tested.

James Russell Lowell

CHAPTER TWENTY-THREE

THE RIVER OF DIFFICULTY

A very tired traveller came to the banks of a river.

There was no bridge by which he could cross. It was winter, and the surface of the river was covered with ice. It was getting dark, and he wanted to reach the other side while there was enough light to see. He debated about whether or not the ice would bear his weight.

Finally, after much hesitation and fear, he got down on his knees and began very cautiously to creep across the surface of the ice. He hoped that by distributing the weight of his body, the ice would be less apt to break under the load.

After he made his slow and painful journey about halfway across the river, he suddenly heard the sound of singing behind him. Out of the dusk, there came a 4-horse load of coal driven by a man singing merrily as he went to his carefree way. Here was the traveller, fearfully inching his way on his hands and knees. And there, as if whisked along by the winter's wind, went the driver, his horses, his sled, and the heavy load of coal over the same river!

Anxiety magnifies the problems in your mind and makes a mountain out of a molehill.

CHAPTER TWENTY-FOUR

TRULY YOURS

A man died, when he realized it, he saw God coming closer with a suitcase in his hand.

God said: Alright son it is time to go.

Surprised the man responded: Now? So soon? I had a lot of plans.

God: I'm sorry but it is time to go.

Man: What do you have in that suitcase?

God answered: Your belongings.

Man: My belongings? You mean my things, my clothes, and my money?

God answered: Those things were not yours they belonged to the earth.

Man: Is it my memories?

God answered: Those never belonged to you - they belonged to Time

Man: Is it my talents?

God answered: Those were never yours - they belonged to the circumstances.

Man: Is it my friends and family?

God answered: I'm sorry they were never yours they belonged to the path.

Man: Is it my wife and son?

God answered: They were never yours they belonged to your heart.

Man: Is it my body?

God answered: that was never yours it belonged to the dust.

Man: Is it my soul?

God answered: No that is mine.

Full of fear, the man took the suitcase from god and opened it just to find out the suitcase was empty.

With a tear coming down his cheek the man said: I never had anything?

God answered: That is correct, what was truly yours was every moment you lived! Life is just a moment - a moment that belonged to you. This is why you should enjoy every moment and not let anything that you think you own stop you from doing so.

PARADOX

A few centuries ago, a Law teacher came across a student who was willing to learn but was unable to pay the fees.

The student struck a deal saying, "I will pay your fee the day I win my first case in the court."

The teacher agreed and proceeded with the law course. When the course was finished and teacher started pestering the student to pay up the fee, the student reminded him of the deal and pushed days.

Fed up with this, the teacher decided to sue the student in the court of law and both of them decided to argue for themselves.

The teacher put forward his argument saying, "If I win this case, the student has to pay me as the case is about his non-payment of dues. And if I lose the case, student will still pay me because he would have won his first case. So either way I will have to get the money."

The equally brilliant student argued back saying, "If I win the case, as per the court of law, I don't have to pay anything to the teacher as the case is about my non-payment of dues. And if I lose the case, I don't have to pay him because I haven't won my first case yet. Either way, I am not going to pay the teacher anything."

CHAPTER TWENTY-SIX

THE BUDDHA IS ABUSED

Buddha seemed quite unruffled by the insults hurled at him by a visitor. When his disciples later asked him what the secret of his serenity was, he said:

"Imagine what would happen if someone placed an offering before you and you did not pick it up. Or someone sent you a letter that you refused to open; you would be unaffected by its contents, would you not? Do this each time you are abused and you will not lose your serenity."

"To enjoy good health, to bring true happiness to one's family, to bring peace to all; one must first discipline one's own mind. If a man can control his mind, he can find the way to Enlightenment, and all wisdom and virtue will come naturally to him.

The Buddha

CHAPTER TWENTY-SEVEN

A WONDERFUL WORLD

A space traveller in the not-so-distant future having spent many decades living and working on Planet Earth retired and landed back on his home planet.

One of the people who received him at the space station asked him, "It must have been wonderful to live for so many years on a planet that is considered to be one of the most beautiful in the universe."

The space traveller ruminated on the question and answered, "If only I had known that to be the case, I would have actually looked at it and experienced it for myself."

CHAPTER TWENTY-EIGHT

A Buddha is Among You

The abbot of a once famous Buddhist monastery that had fallen into decline was deeply troubled. Monks were lax in their practice; novices were leaving and lay supporters deserting it for other centres. He travelled far to a sage and recounted his tale of woe, of how much he desired to transform his monastery to the flourishing haven it had been in the days of yore.

The sage looked him in the eye and said, "The reason your monastery has languished is that the Buddha is living among you in disguise, and you have not honoured Him."

The abbot hurried back, his mind in turmoil. The Selfless One was at his monastery! Who could He be? Brother Hua? No, he was full of sloth. Brother Po? No, he was too dull. But then the *Tathagata* was in disguise. What better disguise than sloth or dull-wittedness?

He called his monks to him and revealed the sage's words. They, too, were taken aback and looked at each other with suspicion and awe. Which one of them was the Chosen One? The disguise was perfect.

Not knowing who He was they took to treating everyone with the respect due to a Buddha. Their faces started shining with an inner radiance that attracted novices and then lay supporters. In no time at all, the monastery far surpassed its previous glory.

CHAPTER TWENTY-NINE

THE BURDEN

Tanzan and Ekido were once traveling together down a muddy road. A heavy rain was still falling.

Coming around a bend, they met a lovely girl in a silk kimono and sash, unable to cross the intersection.

"Come on, girl" said Tanzan at once. Lifting her in his arms, he carried her over the mud. Ekido did not speak again until that night when they reached a lodging temple. Then he no longer could restrain himself.

"We monks don't go near females," he told Tanzan, "especially not young and lovely ones. It is dangerous. Why did you do that?"

"I left the girl there," said Tanzan. "Are you still carrying her?"

"With integrity, you have nothing to fear, since you have nothing to hide. With integrity, you will do the right thing, so you will have no guilt.

Zig Ziglar

CHAPTER THIRTY

TEMPERAMENT

A Zen student came to Bankei and complained: "Master, I have an uncontrollable temper. How can I cure it?"

"You have something very strange," replied Bankei. "Let me see what you have."

"I cannot show it to you right now" replied the other.

"When can you show it to me?" asked Bankei

"It arises unexpectedly," replied the student.

"Then," concluded Bankei, "it cannot be your own true nature. If it were, you could show it to me any time. When you were born, you did not have it, and your parents did not give it to you. Think that over."

"You will not be punished for your anger, you will be punished by your anger."

The Buddha

CHAPTER THIRTY-ONE

INTEGRITY

A man who was troubled in mind once swore that if his problems were solved, he would sell his house and give all the money gained from it to the poor.

The time came when he realized that he must redeem his oath. But he did not want to give away so much money. So he thought of a way out.

He put the house on sale at one silver piece. Included with the house, however, was a cat. The price asked for this animal was ten thousand pieces of silver.

Another man bought the house and cat. The first man gave the single piece of silver to the poor, and pocketed the ten thousand pieces for himself.

"The weak in courage is strong in cunning."
William Blake

CHAPTER THIRTY-TWO

THE CLOAK

Nasrudin heard that there was a banquet being held in the near-by town, and that everyone was invited. He made his way there as quickly as he could. When the Master of Ceremonies saw him in his ragged cloak, he seated him in the most inconspicuous place far from the great table where the most important people were being waited on hand and foot.

Nasrudin saw that it would be an hour at least before the waiters reached the place where he was sitting, so he got up and went home. He dressed himself in a magnificent sable cloak and turban and returned to the feast. As soon as the heralds of the Emir, his host, saw this splendid sight they started to beat the drum of welcome and sound the trumpets in a manner consonant with a visitor of high rank.

The Chamberlain came out of the palace himself, and conducted the magnificent Nasrudin to a place almost next to the Emir. A dish of wonderful food was immediately placed before him. Without a pause, Nasrudin began to rub handfuls of it into his turban and cloak.

"*Your Eminence*," said the prince," I am curious as to your eating habits, which are new to me."

"Nothing special," said Nasrudin; "the cloak got me in here, got me the food. Surely it deserves its portion?"

CHAPTER THIRTY-THREE

TEETHING TROUBLE

A famous Sufi master was invited to give a course in California.

The auditorium was full at 8AM - the time announced - when one of the assistants came onto the stage. "The master is just waking up. Please be patient."

Time passed, and people started leaving the room. At midday, the assistant returned to the stage, saying that the master would be starting the lecture the minute he finished talking to a pretty girl he had just met.

Most of the remaining audience left.

At 4PM the master appeared - apparently drunk. This time, all but 6 people stormed out.

"I will teach you this," said the master, ceasing to act drunk. "Whoever wishes to go down a long path, must learn that the first lesson is to overcome early disappointments."

CHAPTER THIRTY-FOUR

YOUR GREATEST WEAKNESS

This is a story of one 10-year-old boy who decided to study judo despite the fact that he had lost his left arm in a devastating car accident.

The boy began lessons with an old Japanese judo master. The boy was doing well, so he couldn't understand why, after three months of training, the master had taught him only one move.

"Sensei," the boy finally said, "Shouldn't I be learning more moves?"

"This is the only move you know, but this is the only move you'll ever need to know," the Sensei replied. Not quite understanding, but believing in his teacher, the boy kept training.

Several months later, the Sensei took the boy to his first tournament. Surprising himself, the boy easily won his first two matches. The third match proved to be more difficult, but after some time, his opponent became impatient and charged; the boy deftly used his one move to win the match. Still amazed by his success, the boy was now in the finals.

This time, his opponent was bigger, stronger, and more experienced. For a while, the boy appeared to be overmatched. Concerned that the boy might get hurt, the referee called a time-out. He was about to stop the match when the Sensei intervened. "No," the Sensei insisted, "Let him continue."

Soon after the match resumed, his opponent made a critical mistake: he dropped his guard. Instantly, the boy used his move to pin him. The boy had won the match and the tournament. He was the champion.

On the way home, the boy and Sensei reviewed every move in each and every match. Then the boy summoned the courage to ask what was really on his mind. "Sensei, how did I win the tournament with only one move?"

"You won for two reasons," the Sensei answered. "First, you've almost mastered one of the most difficult throws in all of judo. And second, the only known defence for that move is for your opponent to grab your left arm."

The boy's greatest weakness had become his greatest strength.

"Simulated disorder postulates perfect discipline; simulated fear postulates courage; simulated weakness postulates strength.

Lao Tzu

~

BEING LIVELY

The Japanese have always loved fresh fish. But the waters close to Japan have not held many fish for decades. So to feed the Japanese population, fishing boats got bigger and went farther than ever. The farther the fishermen went, the longer it took to bring in the fish. If the return trip took more than a few days, the fish were not fresh. The Japanese did not like the taste.

To solve this problem, fishing companies installed freezers on their boats. They would catch the fish and freeze them at sea. Freezers allowed the boats to go farther and stay longer. However, the Japanese could taste the difference between fresh and frozen and they did not like frozen fish. The frozen fish brought a lower price.

So fishing companies installed fish tanks. They would catch the fish and stuff them in the tanks. After a little thrashing around, the fish stopped moving. They were tired and dull, but alive. Unfortunately, the Japanese could still taste the difference. Because the fish did not move for days, they lost their fresh-fish taste.

The Japanese preferred the lively taste of fresh fish, not sluggish fish. So how did Japanese fishing companies solve this problem? How do they get fresh-tasting fish to Japan? How did the Japanese managed to keep the fish fresh?

To keep the fish tasting fresh, the Japanese fishing companies still put the fish in the tanks. But now they add a small shark to each tank. The shark eats a few fish, but most of the fish arrive in a very lively state. The fish are challenged.

CHAPTER THIRTY-SIX

BELIEF

As a drought continued for what seemed an eternity, a small community of farmers was in a quandary as to what to do. Rain was important to keep their crops healthy and sustain the towns' way of life.

As the problem became more acute, a local pastor called a prayer meeting to ask for rain.

Many people arrived. The pastor greeted most of them as they filed in. As he walked to the front of the church to officially begin the meeting he noticed most people were chatting across the aisles and socializing with friends.

When he reached the front his thoughts were on quieting the attendees and starting the meeting. His eyes scanned the crowd as he asked for quiet. He noticed an eleven year-old girl sitting quietly in the front row. Her face was beaming with excitement. Next to her, poised and ready for use, was a bright red umbrella. The little girl's beauty and innocence made the pastor smile as he realized how much faith she possessed. No one else in the congregation had brought an umbrella.

All came to pray for rain, but the little girl had come prepared, because she believed!

"Faith is the bird that feels the light when the dawn is still dark.

Rabindranath Tagore

CHAPTER THIRTY-SEVEN

HANG THEM UP

I hired a carpenter to help me restore an old farmhouse. He had a rough first day on the job. A flat tire made him lose an hour of work, his electric saw quit, and now his ancient pickup truck refused to start. While I drove him home, he sat in stony silence.

On arriving, he invited me in to meet his family. As we walked toward the front door, he paused briefly at a small tree, touching the tips of some branches with both hands. As he opened the door, he underwent an amazing transformation. His tanned face was wreathed in smiles and he hugged his two small children and gave his wife a kiss.

Afterward he walked me to the car. We passed the tree and my curiosity got the better of me. I asked him about what I had seen him do earlier.

"Oh, that's my trouble tree," he replied. "I know I can't help having troubles on the job, but one thing's for sure, troubles don't belong in the house with my wife and the children.

So, I just hang them up on the tree every night when I come home. Then in the morning I pick them up again."

Then he smiled and said, "Funny thing is, when I come out in the morning to pick 'em up, there aren't nearly as many as I remember hanging up the night before."

CHAPTER THIRTY-EIGHT

PROGRAMMED

A man was spending his holiday in Africa. One day he watched the elephants passing by. To his great surprise these giant strong animals were being held only by a small rope, tied to their front leg. Obviously, they could easily run away any moment. However, they did not.

Then he saw a trainer and asked him, how could this happen that not a single elephant makes an attempt to break free.

The trainer explained, "When the elephants are very young, we use the same size rope to tie them, and at that time it is enough to hold them. Gradually they grow up, get stronger, nevertheless they never try to get away, as they believe that the rope will still hold them."

The man was stunned. These strong animals could break free any time, but they did not, because they believed that this is impossible.

How many of us go through life hanging onto a belief that we cannot do something, simply because we failed at it once before?easier

CHAPTER THIRTY-NINE

THE POWER OF THOUGHT

One man was travelling and suddenly he got to the paradise.

He sat down under the desire tree (there is such tree in *Paradise*, sitting under which you can immediately fulfil any your desire, you just need to think about it) and thought: "I am hungry, so it would be nice to have a bite right now." And when he just thought about this, a table full of different dishes that he was thinking about appeared right before him.

Wow! – The man was surprised, – but it can't be! – He thought so, and the table with dishes disappeared immediately. "It would be nice to get it back!" – And dishes appeared again. He ate plenty of dishes – he had never eaten such tasty food before. After satisfying hunger he thought: it would be nice to drink something – and some perfect wine appeared immediately, because there are no restrictions in the paradise.

Lying in the shadow of the tree and drinking wine, he started wondering: Why do these miracles happen? It just can't be that everything would be so good – probably some ghosts are playing a joke on me.

Suddenly the ghosts appeared. They were terrible – just as he had imagined them to be. The man became scared and thought: Now they will kill me!

And they did.

We produce 60,000 thoughts each day! They are responsible for our happiness and our distress.

Easier to Judge

Once upon a time there was a painter who had just completed his course. He took 3 days and painted beautiful scenery. He wanted people's opinion about his calibre and painting skills.

He put his creation at a busy street-crossing. And just down below a board which read -"I have painted this piece. Since I'm new to this profession I might have committed some mistakes in my strokes etc. Please put a cross wherever you see a mistake."

While he came back in the evening to collect his painting he was completely shattered to see that whole canvass was filled with Xs (crosses) and some people had even written their comments on the painting.

Disheartened and broken completely he ran to his master's place and burst into tears.

This young artist was breathing heavily and master heard him saying, "I'm useless and if this is what I have learnt to paint I'm not worth becoming a painter. People have rejected me completely. I feel like dying"

Master smiled and suggested "My Son, I will prove that you are a great artist and have learnt flawless painting. Do as I say without questioning it. It WILL work."

Young artist reluctantly agreed and two days later early morning he presented a replica of his earlier painting to his master. Master took that gracefully and smiled.

"Come with me" master said.

They reached the same street-square early morning and displayed the same painting exactly at the same place. Now master took out another board which read - "Gentlemen, I have painted this piece. Since I'm new to this profession I might have committed some mistakes in my strokes etc. I have put a box with colors and brushes just below. Please do a favor. If you see a mistake, kindly pick up the brush and correct it."

Master and disciple walked back home.

They both visited the place same evening. Young painter was surprised to see that actually there was not a single correction done so far. Next day again they visited and found painting remained untouched. They say the painting was kept there for a month for no correction came in!

"It behoves every man to remember that the work of a critic is of altogether secondary importance, and that, in the end, progress is accomplished by the man who does things.

Theodore Roosevelt

EXCELLENCE

A tourist once visited a temple under construction where he saw a sculptor making an idol of God. Suddenly he noticed a similar idol lying nearby.

Surprised, he asked the sculptor, "Do you need two statues of the same idol?"

"No," said the sculptor without looking up, "We need only one, but the first one got damaged at the last stage." The gentleman examined the idol and found no apparent damage.

"Where is the damage?" he asked.

"There is a scratch on the nose of the idol." said the sculptor, still busy with his work.

"Where are you going to install the idol?"

The sculptor replied that it would be installed on a pillar twenty feet high. "If the idol is that far, who is going to know that there is a scratch on the nose?" the gentleman asked.

The sculptor stopped his work, looked up at the gentleman, smiled and said, "I will know it."

NEITHER HERE NOR THERE

This Akbar - Birbal story is just one of the many stories, which are an integral part of rich Indian heritage.

The wisdom of Birbal was unparalleled during the reign of Emperor Akbar. But Akbar's brother in law was extremely jealous of him. He asked the Emperor to dispense with Birbal's services and appoint him in his place. He gave ample assurance that he would prove to be more efficient and capable than Birbal. Before Akbar could take a decision on this matter, this news reached Birbal.

Birbal resigned and left. Akbar's brother in law was made the minister in place of Birbal. Akbar decided to test the new minister. He gave three hundred gold coins to him and said, "Spend these gold coins such that, I get a hundred gold coins here in this life; a hundred gold coins in the other world and another hundred gold coins neither here nor there."

The minister found the entire situation to be a maze of confusion and hopelessness. He spent sleepless nights worrying over how he would get himself out of this mess. Thinking in circles was making him go crazy. Eventually, on the advice of his wife he sought Birbal's help. Birbal said, "Just give me the gold cons. I shall handle the rest."

Birbal walked the streets of the city holding the bag of gold coins in his hand. He noticed a rich merchant celebrating his son's wedding. Birbal gave a hundred gold coins to him and bowed courteously saying, "The Emperor Akbar sends you his good wishes and blessings for the wedding of your son. Please accept the gift he has sent." The merchant felt honoured that the king had sent a special messenger with such a precious gift. He honoured Birbal and gave him a large number of expensive gifts and a bag of gold coins as a return gift for the king.

Next, Birbal went to the area of the city were the poor people lived. There he bought food and clothing in exchange for a hundred gold coins and distributed them in the name of the Emperor.

When he came back to town he organized a concert of music and dance. He spent a hundred gold coins on it.

The next day Birbal entered Akbar's darbar and announced that he had done all that the king had asked his brother-in-law to do. The Emperor waited to know how he had done it.

Birbal repeated the sequences of all the events and then said, "The money I gave to the merchant for the wedding of his son – you have got back while on this earth. The money I spent on buying food and clothing for the poor – you will get it in the other world. The money I spent on the musical concert – you will get neither here nor there.

CHAPTER FORTY-THREE

THE GLITTERING NECKLACE

Once there was a king who had presented his daughter, the princess, with a beautiful diamond necklace. The necklace was stolen and his people in the kingdom searched everywhere but could not find it. Some said a bird may have stolen it. The king then asked them all to search for it and put a reward for 50,000 gold coins for anyone who found it.

One day a clerk was walking home along a river next to an industrial area. This river was completely polluted and filthy and smelly. As he was walking, the clerk saw a shimmering in the river and when he looked, he saw the diamond necklace. He decided to try and catch it so that he could get the 50,000 gold coin reward.

He put his hand in the filthy, dirty river and grabbed at the necklace, but somehow missed it and didn't catch it. He took his hand out and looked again and the necklace was still there. He tried again, this time he walked in the river and dirtied his pants in the filthy river and put his whole arm in to catch the necklace. But strangely, he still missed the necklace! He came out and started walking away, feeling depressed.

After some time, he came back again and saw the necklace, right there. This time he was determined to get it, no matter what. He decided to plunge into the river, although it was a disgusting thing to do as the river was polluted, and his whole body would become filthy. He plunged in, and searched everywhere for the necklace and yet he failed.

This time he was really bewildered and came out feeling very depressed that he could not get the necklace that would get him the reward.

Just then a saint who was walking by, saw him, and asked him what the matter was.

The clerk didn't want to share the secret with the saint, thinking the saint might take the necklace for himself, so he refused to tell the saint anything.

But the saint could see this man was troubled and being compassionate, again asked the clerk to tell him the problem and promised that he would not tell anyone about it. The clerk mustered some courage and decided to put some faith in the saint.

He told the saint about the necklace and how he tried and tried to catch it, but kept failing. The saint then told him that perhaps he should try looking upward, toward the branches of the tree, instead of in the filthy river.

The clerk looked up and truly enough, the necklace was dangling on the branch of a tree. He had been trying to capture a mere reflection of the real necklace all this time.

HALF FULL OR HALF EMPTY

A king in Africa had a close friend he grew up with. The friend had a habit of looking at every situation that ever occurred in his life (positive or negative) and remarking, "This is good!"

One day the king and his friend were out on a hunting expedition. The friend would load and prepare the guns for the king. The friend had apparently done something wrong in preparing one of the guns, for after taking the gun from his friend, the king fired it and his thumb was blown off.

Examining the situation the friend remarked as usual, "This is good!" To which the king replied, "No, this is NOT good!" and had his friend sent to jail.

About a year later, the king was hunting in an area that he should have known to stay clear of. Cannibals captured him and took them to their village. They tied his hands, stacked some wood, set up a stake and bound him to the stake. As they came near to set fire to the wood, they noticed that the king was missing a thumb.

Being superstitious, they never ate anyone that was less than whole. So untying the king, they sent him on his way. As he returned home, he was reminded of the event that had taken his thumb and felt remorse for his treatment of his friend.

He went immediately to the jail to speak with his friend. "You were right" he said, "it was good that my thumb was blown off." And he proceeded to tell his friend all that had just happened. "And so I am very sorry for sending you to jail for so long. It was bad for me to do this."

"No," his friend replied, "this is good!"

"What do you mean, 'This is good?!' How could it be good that I sent my friend to jail for a year?"

"If I had not been in jail, I would have been with you!"

"You cannot connect the dots looking forward; you can only connect them looking backward. So you have to trust that the dots will somehow connect in the future. You have to trust in something – your gut, destiny, karma, life, whatever. This approach has never let me down, and it has made all the difference in my life.

Steve Jobs

THE BICYCLE

A Zen Teacher saw five of his students return from the market, riding their bicycles. When they had dismounted, the teacher asked the students, "Why are you riding your bicycles?"

The first student replied, "The bicycle is carrying this sack of potatoes. I am glad that I do not have to carry them on my back!"

The teacher praised the student, saying, "You are a smart boy. When you grow old, you will not walk hunched over, as I do."

The second student replied, "I love to watch the trees and fields pass by as I roll down the path."

The teacher commended the student, "Your eyes are open and you see the world."

The third student replied, "When I ride my bicycle, I am content to chant, *nam myoho renge kyo.*"

The teacher gave praise to the third student, "Your mind will roll with the ease of a newly trued wheel."

The fourth student answered, "Riding my bicycle, I live in harmony with all beings."

The teacher was pleased and said, "You are riding on the golden path of non-harming."

The fifth student replied, "I ride my bicycle to ride my bicycle."

The teacher went and sat at the feet of the fifth student, and said, "I am your disciple."

PAINTING THE WORLD GREEN

There was a millionaire who was bothered by severe eye pain. He consulted so many physicians and was getting his treatment done. He did not stop consulting galaxy of medical experts; he consumed heavy loads of drugs and underwent hundreds of injections.

But the ache persisted with great vigour than before. At last a monk who has supposed to be an expert in treating such patients was called for by the millionaire. The monk understood his problem and said that for sometime he should concentrate only on green colours and not to fall his eyes on any other colours.

The millionaire got together a group of painters and purchased barrels of green color and directed that every object his eye was likely to fall to be painted in green colour just as the monk had directed.

When the monk came to visit him after few days, the millionaire's servants ran with buckets of green paints and poured on him since he was in red dress, lest their master not see any other colour and his eye ache would come back.

Hearing this monk laughed said "If only you had purchased a pair of green spectacles, worth just a few rupees, you could have saved these walls and trees and pots and all other articles and also could have saved a large share of his fortune. You cannot paint the world green!"

SHAKE IT OFF AND STEP UP

One day a farmer's donkey fell down into a well. The animal cried piteously for hours as the farmer tried to figure out what to do. Finally, he decided the animal was old, and the well needed to be covered up anyway; it just wasn't worth it to retrieve the donkey. He invited all his neighbours to come over and help him. They all grabbed a shovel and began to shovel dirt into the well.

At first, the donkey realized what was happening and cried horribly. Then, to everyone's amazement he quieted down.

A few shovel loads later, the farmer finally looked down the well. He was astonished at what he saw. with each shovel of dirt that hit his back, the donkey was doing something amazing. He would shake it off and take a step up. As the farmer's neighbours continued to shovel dirt on top of the animal, he would shake it off and take a step up. Pretty soon, everyone was amazed as the donkey stepped up over the edge of the well and happily trotted off!

Life is going to shovel dirt on you, all kinds of dirt. Learn to shake it off and step up!

EMPATHY

A surgeon entered the hospital in a tearing hurry after being called in for an urgent surgery. He made a note in the register, quickly changed his clothes and then went directly to the operation theatre.

He found the boy's father pacing in the hall waiting for the surgeon.

On seeing him, the boy's father yelled, "Why did you take so long to come? Don't you know that my son's life is in danger? Don't you surgeons have any sense of responsibility?"

The doctor smiled sadly, "I am sorry, I wasn't in the hospital and I came as fast as I could after receiving the call. I just couldn't have come any sooner than this. Now please calm down so that I can do my work."

"Calm down! What if it was your son was in this room right now, would you calm down? If your own son dies now what will you do?" said the father in rage.

The doctor smiled, "I can understand your helplessness and frustration. We doctors cannot perform miracles. We will do our best with God's grace."

"It is so easy to advise when you are not personally affected, isn't it?" murmured the father.

As the surgeon entered the operation theatre and the door was shut and bolted, the angry father turned to the nurse, "Why is he so arrogant?"

The nurse answered, tears streaming down her face, "His son was killed yesterday in a road accident, he was at the burial when we called him for your son's surgery. He could have refused, but he realized that it was a human life at stake and no other surgeon with the same expertise was readily available, so he agreed. Thereafter, he rushed here as fast as he could. No doubt his family would be extremely unhappy with his decision."

The silence was deafening!

"Empathy begins with understanding life from another person's perspective. Nobody has an objective experience of reality. It is all through our own individual prisms.

Sterling K Brown

CHARITY WRAPPED IN DIGNITY

She asked him, "How much are you selling the eggs for?"

The old seller replied to her, "Rs.5/- for one egg, Madam."

She said to him, "I will take 6 eggs for Rs.25/- or I will leave."

The old seller replied reluctantly, "Okay, madam. Please take them. Sales have not been so good today and I have little choice."

She took it and walked away with a feeling of pride that she had a good bargain. She got into her fancy car and went to pick her friend, and invited her to a posh restaurant.

She and her friend sat down and ordered what they liked. They ate a little and left a lot of what they ordered.

The bill was presented for Rs. 4,760.

She paid Rs. 5000 and said, "Keep the change!"

CHAPTER FIFTY

PARTIAL KNOWLEDGE

One day an aeroplane cleaner was cleaning the pilots' cockpit when he saw a book titled: How to Fly an Aeroplane? For Beginners - Volume One

He opened the first page which said: To start the engine, press the red button. He did so and the airplane engine started.

He was happy and opened the next page: To set airplane moving press the blue button.

He did so and the aeroplane started moving at an amazing speed.

He wanted to fly so he opened the third page which read - To let the aeroplane fly, please press the green button.

He did this and the plane started to fly.

He was excited!

After 20 minutes of flying, he was satisfied and wanted to land so he decided to go to the fourth page.

The fourth page read: To learn how to land, please purchase Volume Two at the nearest bookshop!

CHAPTER FIFTY-ONE

OBSTACLES

Once upon an ancient time, a king had a boulder placed on a roadway. Then he hid himself and watched to see if anyone would remove the huge rock.

Some of the king's wealthiest merchants and courtiers came by and simply walked around it.

Many loudly blamed the king for not keeping the roads clear, but none did anything about getting the big stone out of the way.

Then a peasant came along carrying a load of vegetables. On approaching the boulder, the peasant laid down his burden and tried to move the stone to the side of the road.

After strenuous efforts, he finally succeeded. Many others had passed by, they simply mocked him for his efforts and walked around, but not one stopped to help him.

As the peasant picked up his load of vegetables, he noticed a purse lying in the road where the boulder had been. The purse had apparently been placed under the boulder.

The purse contained a note from the king along with several gold coins. The note simply stated that the gold belonged to the person who removed the obstacle.

Every obstacle presents an opportunity to improve one's condition, provided we see it.

CHAPTER FIFTY-TWO

PRIORITY CHECK

The story is told of a woman who bought a parrot to keep her company, but she returned it the next day.

"This bird doesn't talk," she told the owner.

"Does he have a mirror in his cage?" he asked. "Parrots love mirrors. They see their reflection and start conversation."

The woman bought a mirror and left. The next day she returned; the bird still wasn't talking.

"How about a ladder? Parrots love ladders. The happy parrot is a talkative parrot."

The woman bought a ladder and left. But the next day, she was back.

"Does your parrot have a swing? No? Well, that's the problem. Once he starts swinging, he'll talk up a storm."

The woman reluctantly bought a swing and left. When she walked into the store the next day, her countenance had changed.

"The parrot died," she said.

The pet store owner was shocked.

"I'm so sorry. Tell me, did he ever say anything?" he asked.

"Yes, right before it died," the woman replied.

"In a weak voice, it asked me, 'Don't they sell any food at that pet store?'"

Sometimes we forget what's really important in life. Do a 'priority check'.

CHAPTER FIFTY-THREE

THE CHALLENGE

Once Iswarchandra Vidyasagar asked Michael Madhusudan, "Can you make a full paragraph without the letter 'E'"?

Michael Madhusudan answered,

"I doubt if I can. It's an intrinsic part of many, many words. Omitting it is as hard as making muffins without flour. It's as hard as spitting without saliva, napping without a pillow, driving a train without tracks, sailing to Russia without a boat, washing your hands without soap. Anyway, what would I gain? An award? A cash bonus? Bragging rights? Why should I sprain my brain? It's not worth it."

CHAPTER FIFTY-FOUR

PEACE

Once there was a king who offered a prize to the artist who would paint the best picture of peace.

Many artists tried.

The king looked at all the pictures. But there were only two he really liked, and he had to choose between them.

One picture was of a calm lake. The lake was a perfect mirror for the towering mountains all around it. Overhead was a blue sky with fluffy white clouds. All who saw this picture thought that it was a perfect picture of peace.

The other picture had mountains, too. But these were rugged and bare. Above was an angry sky, from which rain fell and in which lightning played. Down the side of the mountain tumbled a foaming waterfall. This did not look peaceful at all.

But when the king looked closely, he saw behind the waterfall a tiny bush growing in a crack in the rock. In the bush a mother bird had built her nest. There, in the midst of the rush of angry water, sat the mother bird in her nest — in perfect peace.

Which picture do you think won the prize?

The king chose the second picture.

Do you know why?

"Because," explained the king, "peace does not mean to be in a place where there is no noise, trouble, or hard work. Peace means to be in the midst of all those things and still be calm in your heart. That is the real meaning of peace."

The peace that we seek is not the peace of the graveyard. The real peace is the serenity and tranquillity within, when there is chaos all around us.

"Ego says – Once everything falls into place, I will feel inner peace. Spirit says – Find your inner peace and then everything will fall into place.

Marianne Williamson

CHAPTER FIFTY-FIVE

MAKING THE MOST OF WHAT YOU HAVE

Adjacent to where I stay, a building was being constructed. Lots of daily wage labourers were employed by the civil engineers. Typically, whilst the men undertook the civil work like erecting columns, slabs, floors, etc., the women also worked on carrying bricks, sand and cement to the site; their children hovered around playing.

One of their favourite games was playing 'train-train'. They held on to the shirt-tails of the child in front of them and ran around. One of them would become the engine and others would become bogies. Each day these children took turns becoming the engine and bogies.

But there was one small boy, always clad in a pair of shorts and nothing else, who with the help of one small green cloth which he held in his hand, became the guard on every occasion.

Out of sheer curiosity, I asked him, "Sonny, don't you like to become an engine or a bogey some time?"

The little boy replied softly, "Sir, I don't have a shirt to wear so how will the other children catch me to make the train?"

CHAPTER FIFTY-SIX

PROBLEM VS OPPORTUNITY

In the previous century, two salesmen were sent by one of the popular shoe manufacturing companies to Africa. Their objective was to examine whether or not there was a market for shoes in Africa.

The first salesman reported – "There is no market there – nobody wears shoes."

The second salesman reported – "There is a huge market there – nobody wears shoes."

"Opportunity does not knock, it presents itself when you beat down the door.

Kyle Chandler

CHAPTER FIFTY-SEVEN

PERCEPTION

A famous man was writing his autobiography, he wrote:

- Last year, I had a surgery and my gall bladder was removed. I was bed ridden due to this surgery for a long time.
- I turned sixty and had to give up my favourite job. I spent 30 years of my life in this company.
- My father died.
- My son failed in his examination because he met with a car accident. He had to be hospitalized for weeks. The car was totally destroyed.
- Alas! It was such a bad year.

When his spouse entered the room, she happened to read what was written. She left the room silently and returned with another piece of paper which was placed alongside.

The original writer found this:

- Last year, I finally got rid of my gall bladder due to which I had spent many years in excruciating pain.
- I turned sixty and retired from my favourite job with perfectly good health. Now I can utilize my time to write something and inspire other human beings.
- My father, who was ninety-five years of age, passed away peacefully in his sleep without any prolonged illness.
- My son was blessed with a new life. My car was destroyed, but my son escaped with reparable injuries.
- This year was a blessing!

CHAPTER FIFTY-EIGHT

THE TWO WOLVES

A wise old man was explaining life to his grandson.

He said, "A fight is going on within me. It is a dreadful battle between two wolves. One wolf is evil – he is the personification of fear, anger, envy, sorrow, greed and lies. The other wolf is good – the personification of joy, peace, love, sharing, kindness and truth. This same fight is going on within you and many others."

The grandson thought for a minute and then inquired, "Which wolf will win, grandpa?"

"The one you feed."

CHAPTER FIFTY-NINE

CONDITIONING

In an experiment, a scientist placed a number of fleas in a glass jar. They quickly jumped out, since fleas are capable of jumping several times their height.

He then put the fleas back into the jar and placed a glass lid on top of the jar. When the fleas jumped, they hit the glass lid and fell back into the jar. After a while, the fleas began to jump slightly below the glass in order to avoid hitting it.

After a couple of hours, the scientist removed the glass lid. Yet, the fleas continued jumping below the height of the glass lid. They had learned (conditioning) to stop themselves from jumping beyond the height of the glass lid.

Now, no matter whether the lid is there or not, the fleas will stay in the jar forever. When the fleas produce their offspring, the babies too will copy their behaviour and not jump any higher.

Do we, like the fleas, set limits to what we can achieve? We don't jump as high as we can.

CHAPTER SIXTY

BE DEAF!

Some frogs arranged a contest – to climb to the summit of a very tall tower. Many frogs gathered to witness the contest, although only a few of them participated.

The contest began. The crowd just could not believe that any of their own could possibly reach the summit of the tower. They exclaimed, "It is too difficult!", "No one can possibly make it to the top!", "The tower is too high!" and so on.

The frogs which tried began falling, one after the other. As the crowd continued to demotivate, more frogs just gave up. Those who endeavoured to attempt failed. But one stood apart, after a massive effort, he made it to the summit!

The crowd was astonished. Everyone wanted to know how on earth the frog managed to accomplish this near impossible feat.

The frog was deaf and completely oblivious to the general opinion that it was impossible and could not be done.

CHAPTER SIXTY-ONE

WHEN THE WORLD SAYS NO

When Surendra was a young boy in school, he learnt a lesson in self-confidence.

One day, his English teacher called him to recite a poem in front of the class. He had hardly said a few lines when his teacher interrupted him with a loud 'NO'. Slightly shaken, he began again only to be interrupted once more. He started over and over a few more times, each time the teacher shouted 'NO'. Surendra gave up embarrassed and ashamed.

The teacher now asked Dhirendra to recite the poem. As in the case of Surendra, he had hardly said a few lines when his teacher interrupted him with a loud 'NO'. Dhirendra kept going and did not pause. His teacher shouted 'NO' on a couple of more occasions, but Dhirendra just kept going without a pause.

As he sat down, the teacher said, "Very Good!" and the class applauded.

An irritated Surendra complained, "Teacher, I recited just as he did, every word was correct."

The teacher replied, "It is not enough to know your lesson, you must be one hundred per cent confident and sure. When you allowed me to stop you or make you pause or restart from the beginning, it meant that you were unsure of yourself. When the world says 'NO', it is our business to say 'YES' and prove it!"

CHAPTER SIXTY-TWO

SELF-BELIEF

John Smith was caught in a debt trap and bankruptcy and ruin stared him in the face, if he couldn't find a way out. His creditors were hounding him, demanding to be paid. His bankers were threatening to withdraw the facilities that had been granted to him. His team of loyal employees wanted a pay rise that he couldn't afford. Wearily, unable to find a way out of his predicament, John sat down on a bench in the park lost in own morbid thoughts.

"Hi", said a voice close to him.

John looked up to find an old man sitting next to him. He hadn't noticed, so lost was he in his own thoughts.

"Something seems to be troubling you, sonny?" asked the old man, kindly.

John did not quite know why, but he narrated his ordeal to the old man, who listened patiently.

To his surprise, the old man said, "I can help you."

He pulled a cheque book out of his pocket, wrote something on it, signed it and handed it over to John. He said, "Take this. Meet me here exactly one year from today. And you can pay be back at that time. Wish you good luck." And he walked away, quite briskly for his age.

John looked at the cheque and his eyes went wide when he realized it was for a million dollars, signed by Warren Buffet, one of the richest men in the world.

"I can solve all my problems immediately," he thought aloud, "but I should be careful that I do the right thing so that I can repay him after one year."

After some deliberation, he decided he would not deposit the cheque in his bank, but keep it in the safe to be used only in case of an absolute emergency. His gloomy demeanour was now transformed into an energetic enthusiasm, as he worked harder than before to grab many big orders. He also convinced a few of his buyers to pay him an advance promising a discount and early delivery.

Within a few months, he was rid of his debt in its entirety, had honoured all the commitments to the bank, and managed to give a generous pay rise to his loyal staff. Life was good.

Exactly one year later, he returned to the park bench to find the old man patiently waiting for him. Just as he was about to return the cheque to the old man, a nurse came running and grabbed the old man.

"I hope he hasn't bothered you. He keeps escaping from the sanatorium and tells people he is Warren Buffet," she said, as she led the old man away.

John stood rooted to the spot surprised and shocked as he watched the old man being led away. For a year, he had kept that cheque carefully in a safe, it had transformed his self-belief and his self-confidence.

It is not always money that turns our life around.

CHAPTER SIXTY-THREE

WINNING OVER A FOE

A farmer in ancient China had a neighbour who was a hunter, and who owned ferocious and badly trained hunting dogs. They jumped over the fence frequently and chased the farmer's lambs.

The farmer, on several occasions, requested his neighbour to keep his dogs in check, but this plea fell on deaf ears.

One day the dogs again jumped the fence, attacked and severely injured several lambs, causing a great deal of anguish for the farmer.

The farmer had had enough, and went downtown to consult the local magistrate who listened carefully to the story and said: "I could punish the hunter and instruct him to keep his dogs chained or lock them up. But you would lose a friend and gain an enemy. Which would you rather have, friend or foe for a neighbour?"

The farmer replied that he preferred a friend.

"Alright, I will offer you a solution that keeps your lambs safe, and which will retain your neighbour as a friend."

Having heard the magistrate's solution, the farmer agreed. Once at home, the farmer immediately put the judge's suggestions to the test.

He took three of his best lambs and presented them to his neighbour's three young sons, who were beside themselves with joy and began to play with them. To protect his son's newly acquired playthings, the hunter built a strong kennel for his dogs. He also ensured that they were thoroughly trained to obey and did not show any aggression except when the master desired it specifically.

Since then, the dogs never again bothered the farmer's lambs. Out of gratitude for the farmer's generosity toward his sons, the hunter often shared the game he had hunted. The farmer reciprocated by sending the hunter the cheese he had made. Within a short time the neighbours became good friends.

One can win over and influence people the best with gestures of kindness and compassion. – An old Chinese saying

One catches more flies with honey than with vinegar. – An old Western saying

CHAPTER SIXTY-FOUR

THE HOLE IN THE BOAT

A man was asked to paint a boat. He brought with him paint and brushes and began to paint the boat a bright red, as the owner asked him. Whilst painting, he noticed that there was a small hole in the hull, and decided to quietly repair it.

When finished painting, he received his money and left. The next day, the owner of the boat came to the painter and presented him with a nice cheque, much higher than the payment for painting.

The painter was surprised and said "You've already paid me for painting the boat Sir!"

"But this is not for the paint job. It's for having repaired the hole in the boat."

"Ah! But it was such a small service, certainly it's not worth paying me such a high amount for something so insignificant."

"My dear friend, you do not understand. Let me tell you what happened. When I asked you to paint the boat, I forgot to mention about the hole. When the boat dried, my kids took the boat and went on a fishing trip. They did not know that there was a hole. I was not at home at that time. When I returned and noticed they had taken the boat, I was desperate because I remembered that the boat had a hole. Imagine my relief and joy when I saw them returning from fishing."

"Then, I examined the boat and found that you had repaired the hole! You see, now, what you did? You saved the life of my children! I do not have enough money to pay your 'small' good deed."

Keep repairing 'boat-holes' along this journey called life, you get surprise rewards.

CHAPTER SIXTY-FIVE

THE VALUE OF LIFE

A little boy went to his grandfather and asked, "What's the value of life?"

The grandpa gave him a red stone and said, "Find out the value of this stone, but don't sell it."

The boy took the stone to an Orange Seller and asked him what its cost would be.

The Orange Seller saw the shiny stone and said, "I can give you two dozen oranges in exchange for the stone." The boy apologized and said that the grandpa has asked him not to sell it.

He went ahead and found a vegetable seller. "What could be the value of this stone?" he asked the vegetable seller.

The seller saw the shiny stone and said, "Take two sacks of potatoes and give me the stone." The boy again apologized and said he can't sell it.

Further ahead, he went into a jewellery shop and asked the value of the stone. The jeweller saw the stone under a lens and said, "I'll give you a million rupees for this stone."

When the boy shook his head, the jeweller said, "Alright, alright, let me raise that to two million rupees." The boy explained that he could not sell the stone.

Further ahead, the boy saw a boutique shop, which only dealt with precious stones and asked the seller the value of this stone. When the seller saw the big red ruby, his eyes bulged as he laid it down over a piece of cloth. After examining it thoroughly, he asked, "Where did you get this priceless ruby from? Even if I sell myself and my shop, I won't be able to purchase this priceless stone."

Stunned and confused, the boy returned to the grandfather and told him what had happened. "Now please tell me what all this means and what is the value of life, grandpa."

Grandfather said, "You may be a precious stone, even priceless, but, people will value you based on their financial status, their level of information, their belief in you, and their motive behind entertaining you, their ambition, and their risk taking ability. Yet, you may surely find someone who will discern your true value."

You are unique and priceless. Respect yourself. Don't sell yourself cheap.

CHAPTER SIXTY-SIX

EXPERIENTIAL LEARNING

Parth was the son of a burglar, because that was his father's profession. As a modern day Robinhood, he ensured that his family lived a good comfortable life and he was also charitable, as he distributed his ill-gotten wealth amongst the poor and the needy.

He had never been caught even once. And he was highly respected in the community and the neighbourhood.

One day, realising that his father was growing old, Parth asked him, "Father, teach me your trade so that when you retire, I can carry on the family tradition."

The father did not reply; that night, however, he took his son along with him to break into a house. Once inside he opened a closet and asked his son to search what was inside. No sooner had the young lad stepped inside, his father slammed the door shut and bolted it, making enough commotion in the process to awaken the household. He then slipped quietly away.

The young lad was at first confused, then angry and terrified that his own father could do this to him. Hearing voices outside, his mind then switched to planning his escape. He had an idea – he began to meow like a cat – something he was very good at.

One of the family members or their servants outside lit a candle and opened the closet to let the cat out, relieved that it wasn't a burglar after all. The young lad jumped out the moment the closet door opened and ran for his life. Alarmed, other members in the family gave chase.

Thinking swiftly, the boy spied a well beside the road and threw a large stone into it and quickly hid in the bushes, invisible in the dark. The pursuers heard the loud splash and peered into the dark well, making sure the burglar did not emerge. After watching intently for a few minutes, satisfied that the burglar had drowned, they went away.

The boy waited patiently for another fifteen minutes just to be sure they did not return. He then swiftly made his way back home. Exhausted and excited, forgetting his anger, be blurted out his adventures to his father as to how he had made his escape.

His father merely responded with a smile, "The fact that you are here tells me you have learnt the trade."

"You gain strength, courage and confidence by every experience in which you really stop to look fear in the face. You are able to say to yourself, 'I lived through this horror. I can take the next thing that comes along'.

Eleanor Roosevelt

CHAPTER SIXTY-SEVEN

BE PROACTIVE

Nasruddin handed a young boy a pitcher and told him to go and fetch water from the well. Before the kid set out, however, he slapped him on the ear and shouted, "Be very careful! Mind you don't drop it!"

Said an onlooker, "Pray why do you strike a poor child before he has done anything wrong?"

Replied Nasruddin, "Think for a moment, man. Would you prefer that I strike him *after* icecreamhe has broken the pitcher and spilled the water? Both the pitcher and the water are lost. Now, when I have slapped him, he will remember and both pitcher and water are saved."

CHAPTER SIXTY-EIGHT

THE SHEER FORCE OF HABIT

It is said that when the Great Library of Alexandria was burned down, only one book survived. It was a very ordinary book, not like those who were burnt which had leather binding and gold lettering. This was plain simple paperback, dog eared, and yellowed by age.

When found among the ashes, it was thought to have no value. It was sold for 10 cents to a poor man who barely knew how to read. This plain and common book however was probably the most valuable book in the world. In the last section of the book were a few sentences that pointed to a source of the secret of immortality or eternal life.

This source is a tiny pebble, that if ingested will give the person eternal life! The writing declared that this precious pebble was lying somewhere along the beaches of Desaru, facing the South China Sea in the southern tip of the east coast of Peninsular Malaysia.

This pebble was lying among thousands of pebbles that were exactly like it, except in one aspect- whereas all other pebbles were cold to the touch in the morning; this one will feel warm, almost as if it were alive.

The man rejoiced at his good luck. He sold everything he had, borrowed a large sum of money that would last him for at least a year, booked a room at Desaru Pulai Resort Hotel, and began his search for this priceless pebble. He worked out a search grid and did his search systematically. This is how he did it.

Every morning, he will go to the assigned search area. He would lift a pebble. If it was cold to the touch, he would not throw it back on the shore because if he did that, he might be examining the same stone over and over again. Instead, he would throw the stone into the South China Sea.

So each day for hours he would continue in this routine: pick up a pebble; if it felt cold, throw it into the sea; lift another... and so on, endlessly. He spent a week, a month, a year and finally years on this quest for eternal life. His savings ran out and he borrowed more money. He got a special discount from Desaru Pulai Resort Hotel for being a long staying customer. On and on his search went: lift a pebble, hold it, feel it, if cold, throw it into the sea, lift another. Hour after hour, week after week, day after day.... still no pebble of immortality.

One evening, he picked up a pebble and it was warm to his touch – but through sheer force of habit, he threw it into the South China Sea!

CHAPTER SIXTY-NINE

MEDITATION

A legend has it that there was a sacred temple built on an island near the Indian subcontinent and it held a thousand bells. Bells, big and small, fashioned by the finest craftsman in the world. When the wind blew or a storm raged, all the bells would peal out in a symphony that would send the heart of the hearer into raptures, and put him in a state of divine bliss.

But over the centuries, the island sank into the sea and, with it, the temple bells. Legend states, however, that the bells continued to peel ceaselessly, and could be heard by anyone who cared to listen intently. Inspired by this legend, a young man, who was a spiritual seeker, travelled hundreds of miles, determined to hear those bells.

He sat for days on the shore, facing the vanished island, and listened with determination. But all he could hear was the sound of the sea. He made every effort to block it out. But to no avail; the sound of the sea seemed to flood the world.

He kept at this task for weeks on end. Each time he got disheartened and was about to give up, he would listen to the village elders who spoke with great passion of the mysterious legend. Then his enthusiasm soared, as it would in the heart of a true seeker, only to be discouraged again when weeks of further effort yielded no result.

Finally he decided to give up the attempt. Perhaps he was not destined to hear the bells. Perhaps he was not destined to experience divine bliss. Perhaps the legend was not true. It was his final day, and he went to the shore to say goodbye to the sea and the sky and the wind and the coconut trees. He lay on the sand, and for the first time listened to the sound of the sea. Soon he was so lost in the sound that he was barely conscious of himself, so deep was the silence that the sound produced.

In the very depth of that profound silence, he heard it! The tinkle of a tiny bell followed by another, and another, and another...and soon every one of the thousand temple bells was peeling out in harmony, and his heart leaped in joyous ecstasy as he experienced divine bliss!

CHAPTER SEVENTY

PROBLEM SOLVING

An engineer in a car manufacturing company designed a world class car. The owner was impressed with the outcome and showered praises on him.

However, whilst trying to fetch the vehicle from the manufacturing area out to the office they realised that the car was an inch taller than the entrance.

The engineer was disappointed that he hadn't noticed this before creating the car. The owner was puzzled as to how they were going to bring it out of the manufacturing area.

The painter suggested that they can bring out the car and there would be few scratches on the roof of the car that he will quickly repair in a manner that no one would ever realize. The engineer suggested that they break down the entrance and once the car has been brought out, it can be cemented together again.

The owner wasn't fully convinced – both options seemed a bit unnecessarily destructive to him.

The watchman was watching all these drama and slowly approached the owner, "Sir, may I suggest something?"

"Sure," said the owner, even as the others looked on with contempt.

"Release the air in the tyres and the car can easily be brought out."

All problems don't need to be approached from an expert point of view, sometimes a layman's point of view will suffice.

CHAPTER SEVENTY-ONE

MAKING A DIFFERENCE

This parable was written by Elizabeth Silance Ballard.

It is a story of an elementary teacher. Her name was Mrs. Thompson. And as she stood in front of her 5th grade class on the very first day of school, she told the children a lie. Like most teachers, she looked at her students and said that she loved them all the same. But that was impossible, because there in the front row, slumped in his seat, was a little boy named Teddy Stoddard.

Mrs. Thompson had watched Teddy the year before and noticed that he didn't play well with the other children, that his clothes were messy and that he constantly needed a bath. And Teddy could be unpleasant. It got to the point where Mrs. Thompson would actually take delight in marking his papers with a broad red pen, making bold X's and then putting a big "F" at the top of his papers.

At the school where Mrs. Thompson taught, she was required to review each child's past records and she put

Teddy's off until last. However, when she reviewed his file, she was in for a surprise. Teddy's first grade teacher wrote, "Teddy is a bright child with a ready laugh. He does his work neatly and has good manners; he is a joy to be around."

His second grade teacher wrote, "Teddy is an excellent student, well-liked by his classmates, but he is troubled because his mother has a terminal illness and life at home must be a struggle."

His third grade teacher wrote, "His mother's death has been hard on him. He tries to do his best but his father doesn't show much interest and his home life will soon affect him if some steps aren't taken."

His fourth grade teacher wrote, "Teddy is withdrawn and doesn't show much interest in school. He doesn't have many friends and sometimes sleeps in class." By now, Mrs. Thompson realized the problem and she was ashamed of herself.

She felt even worse when her students brought her Christmas presents wrapped in beautiful ribbons and bright paper, except for Teddy's. His present was clumsily wrapped in the heavy, brown paper that he got from a grocery bag. Mrs. Thompson took pains to open it in the middle of the other presents. Some of the children started to laugh when she found a rhinestone bracelet with some of the stones missing and a bottle that was one quarter full of perfume.

But she stifled the children's laughter when she exclaimed how pretty the bracelet was, putting it on, and dabbing some of the perfume on her wrist. Teddy Stoddard stayed after school that day just long enough to say, "Mrs. Thompson, today you smelled just like my Mom used to." After the children left she cried for at least an hour.

On that very day, she quit teaching reading, and writing and arithmetic. Instead, she began to teach children. Mrs. Thompson paid particular attention to Teddy. As she worked with him, his mind seemed to come alive. The more she encouraged him, the faster he responded. By the end of the year, Teddy had become one of the smartest children in the class and, despite her lie that she would love all the children the same, Teddy became one of her 'teacher's pet'."

A year later, she found a note under her door, from Teddy, telling her that she was still the best teacher he ever had in his whole life. Six years went by before she got another note from Teddy. He then wrote that he had finished high school second in his class, and she was still the best teacher he ever had in his whole life. Four years after that, she got another letter, saying that while things had been tough at times, he'd stayed in school, had stuck with it, and would soon graduate from college with the highest of honours. He assured Mrs. Thompson that she was still the best and favourite teacher he ever had in his whole life.

Then four more years passed and yet another letter came. This time he explained that she was still the best and favourite teacher he ever had. But now his name was a little longer. The letter was signed, *Theodore F. Stoddard, M.D.*

The story doesn't end there. You see, there was yet another letter that spring. Teddy said he'd met this girl and was going to be married. He explained that his father had died a couple of years ago and he was wondering if Mrs. Thompson might agree to sit in the place at the wedding that usually was reserved for the mother of the groom. Of course, Mrs. Thompson did. And guess what? She wore that bracelet, the one with several rhinestones missing. And she made sure she was wearing the perfume that Teddy remembered his mother wearing on their last Christmas together.

They hugged each other, and Dr. Stoddard whispered in Mrs. Thompson's ear, "Thank you, Mrs, Thompson for believing in me. Thank you so much for making me feel important and showing me that I could make a difference."

Mrs. Thompson, with tears in her eyes whispered back. She said, "Teddy, you have it all wrong. You were the one who taught me that I could make a difference. I didn't know how to teach until I met you.

CHAPTER SEVENTY-TWO

THE SMARTEST MAN IN THE WORLD

A doctor, a lawyer, a little boy and a priest were flying on a small private plane. Suddenly, the plane developed engine trouble. In spite of the best efforts of the pilot, the plane started to go down. Finally, the pilot grabbed a parachute and yelled to the passengers that they better jump, and he bailed himself out.

Unfortunately, only three parachutes remained.

The doctor grabbed one of the parachutes and said "I'm a doctor, I save lives, so I must live to save other's lives," and jumped out.

The lawyer then said, "I'm a lawyer and lawyers are the smartest people in the world. I deserve to live." He also grabbed a parachute and jumped.

The priest looked at the little boy and said, "My son, I've lived a long and full life. You are young and have your whole life ahead of you. Take the last parachute and live in peace."

The little boy handed the parachute back to the priest and said, "Do not worry Father. The smartest man in the world just took off with my back pack."

CHAPTER SEVENTY-THREE

DESTINY

A great Japanese warrior named Nobunaga was going to war with a fierce enemy with only one-tenth the number of men the opposition commanded. He knew that he could win the fight with a well-planned strategy, but his soldiers were in doubt.

On the way the leader stopped at a Shinto shrine and told his men: "After my visit to the shrine I will toss a coin. If the head comes, we will win; if tails, we will lose. Destiny holds us in her hand."

Nobunaga entered the shrine and offered his prayers. Then he came forth and tossed a coin in front of his men. Heads appeared. The soldiers were filled with confident and were eager to win the battle.

"No one can change the hand of destiny," one of his attendants told him after the battle.

"Indeed not," said Nobunaga and showed the coin which was doubled with heads on the both side.

CHAPTER SEVENTY-FOUR

LIFE PURPOSE

Once upon a time, there lived a wise man. He was the head of the local administration of a small village. Everyone respected him and his views and opinions were well regarded. Many people came to him seeking for advice.

His son, however, was very lazy and wasted his time sleeping and spending time with his friends. No amount of advice or threat made any difference to him. He wouldn't change at all.

The years passed, and with time faded the youth of the wise man. As he grew older, he began to worry about his son's future. He recognized the need to impart something to his son so that he can take care of himself and his family to be.

One day, he called his son to his room and said- "My son, you are no more a kid now. You must learn to take responsibilities and understand life. I want you to find the real purpose of your life and when you find it, remember it always, and you will lead a life full of happiness and joy."

Then he handed his son a bag. When the son opened the bag, he was surprised to see four pairs of clothes, one for each season. There also were some raw food, grains, lentils, little money and a map. His father continued, "I want you to go find a treasure. I have drawn a map of the place where the treasure is hidden, you need to go and find it."

The son loved this idea. The next day, he eagerly set out on a journey to find the treasure. He had to travel really far across borders, forests, plateaus and mountains. Days turned into weeks and weeks turned into months. Along the way, he met many people. He was helped by some with food and by some with shelter. He also came across robbers who tried to rob him.

Slowly the season changed and so did the landscapes along with it. When the weather was unpleasant, he halted for the day and continued his journey when the weather cleared.

Finally, after a long year, he reached his destination. It was a cliff. The map showed the treasure being placed below the cliff under the tree. Upon spotting the tree, he began to dig the ground. He searched and searched- around it, under it, on it but found nothing. He spent two days looking and digging for the treasure. By the third day, he was so exhausted that he decided to leave.

Disappointed over his father's lie, he headed back to his home. On his way back, he experienced the same changing landscapes and seasons. This time, however, he halted to enjoy the blooming flowers in spring and the dancing birds in monsoon. He stayed in places only to watch the sun set in paradise or to enjoy pleasant summer evenings.

Since, the supplies he carried were over by then, he learned to hunt and make arrangement for his meals. He also learned how to sew his clothes and shelter himself.

He was now able to determine the hour of the day by the position of the sun and plan his journey accordingly. He also learned how to protect himself from wild animals.

He met the same people who had helped him earlier. This time he stayed on for a few days with them and helped them in some or the other way to repay them. He realized how nice they were to a nomadic stranger who had nothing to offer to them in return.

When he reached home, he realized it had been two years since he left the place. He walked straight into his father's room. "Father" He said...

The father immediately jumped to his feet and hugged his son.

"So how was your journey my son, did you find the treasure?" he asked.

"The journey was fascinating father. But forgive me for I wasn't able to find the treasure. Maybe somebody took it before I reached." He surprised himself by what he just said. He wasn't angry at his father. Instead, he was asking for forgiveness.

"There wasn't any treasure in the very first place my son," father answered smiling.

"Why did you send me to find it then?" queried the son.

"I will surely tell you why, but first you tell me, how was your journey to the place? Did you enjoy it?"

"Of course not father! I had no time. I was worried someone else would find the treasure before I did. I was in a hurry to reach the cliff."

He continued "But I did enjoy the journey on my way back home. I made many friends and witnessed miracles every day. I learned so many different skills and the art of survival. There was so much I learnt that it made me forget the pain of not finding the treasure."

The father said to him, "Exactly my son. I do want you to lead your life with a goal. But if you remain too focused on the goal, then you will miss out on the real treasures of life. The truth is, life has no specific goal, other than to just experience it, enjoy the journey, learn and grow every single day."

The purpose of life is to live a life of purpose, whilst enjoying the journey.

CHAPTER SEVENTY-FIVE

PERSPECTIVE

Once there lived a happy couple who had been living happily together for decades. But after spending so many years together, the husband was concerned that his wife was not hearing as well as she used to hear. He thought that she was perhaps in need of a hearing aid but he wasn't quite sure how to approach her on this sensitive subject.

He called his family doctor asked him for a suggestion. The doctor told him to test it with a simple experiment.

The doctor said, "Stand 40 feet away from her and speak as loud as you would speak to her in a normal conversation. Observe if she hears you. If not, reduce the distance to 30 feet, then 20 feet, and so on until you get a response. The distance will help us to ascertain the requirements and specifications for an appropriate hearing aid."

"Thank you so much, Doctor. That's a brilliant idea, I shall try it right away."

The very next day, the husband observed that his wife was cooking lunch in the kitchen. So he took the opportunity to conduct the experiment. He stood 40 feet away from his wife and asked, "Dear, what's for lunch today?" He waited for a response but could not get any.

He moved a bit closer at approximately 30 feet and asked again, "Dear, what is there for lunch?" He still couldn't get any response from his wife.

He then adopted a position approximately 20 feet away from his wife and asked the same question, hoping he would get a response this time. But he failed to gather a response.

He then stood just 10 feet away from his wife and asked "Dear, what is there for lunch?" Even then, he could not garner a response.

By now the husband was deeply concerned and felt a little sad on the state of his beloved wife's hearing ability.

He now walked right up to her and asked, "My dear wife, what's for lunch today?"

The wife shouted, "John, this is the fifth time I'm telling you, CHICKEN!"

CHAPTER SEVENTY-SIX

ENCOURAGEMENT

Dante Gabriel Rossetti, the famous 19th-century poet and artist, was once approached by an elderly man. The old fellow had some sketches and drawings that he wanted Rossetti to look at and tell him if they were any good, or if they at least showed potential talent.

Rossetti looked them over carefully. After the first few, he knew that they were worthless, showing not the least sign of artistic talent. But Rossetti was a kind man, and he told the elderly man as gently as possible that the pictures were without much value and showed little talent. He was sorry, but he could not lie to the man.

The visitor was disappointed, but seemed to expect Rossetti's judgment. He then apologized for taking up Rossetti's time, but would he just look at a few more drawings – the creations of a young art student?

Rossetti looked over the second batch of sketches and immediately became enthusiastic over the talent they revealed. "These," he said, "are quite good. This young student has great talent. He should be given every help and encouragement in his career as an artist. He has a great future if he will work hard and show dedication and perseverance."

Rossetti could see that the old fellow was deeply moved. "Who is this fine young artist?" he asked. "Your son?"

"No," said the old man sadly. "It is me - forty years ago. If only I had heard your praise then! For you see, I got discouraged and gave up - too soon."

CHAPTER SEVENTY-SEVEN

OBSESSIVE COMPULSIVE

A barber was passing under a haunted tree, when he heard a voice say, "Would you like to have the 'Seven Jars of Gold'?"

He looked around and saw no one. Yet his greed was aroused, so he shouted eagerly, "Yes, I certainly would."

"Then go home at once," said the voice, "you will find them there."

The barber ran all the way home. Sure enough, there were the seven jars – all filled with gold, except one which strangely, was only half-full. Now the barber could not bear the thought of having a half-filled jar. He felt an irresistible urge to fill it or he would simply not be happy.

So he had all the jewellery of his family members melted into coins and thrown into the half-filled jar. But the jar remained half-filled! This was exasperating! He saved, scrounged and starved himself and his family. He cut down on expenses. He gave up many things and forced his family to do the same.

Alas! No matter how much gold he poured into the jar, it always remained half-filled.

One day, he got the King to double his salary. So the battle to fill the jar was on again. He even took to begging. The jar devoured every piece of gold that was flung into it, but stubbornly refused to fill.

The King now noticed how starved the barber looked. "What's wrong with you?" he asked, "you used to be so happy when your salary was smaller. Now it has been doubled and you are worn out and dejected. Can it be that you have been given the 'Seven Jars of Gold'?"

The barber was astonished and gave the King a startled look, "Who told you this, Your Majesty?"

The King laughed. "What you display are so obviously the symptoms of the person to whom the ghost has given the seven jars. It once offered them to me. When I asked if the money could be spent or it was merely to be hoarded, it vanished without a word."

The King continued, "That wealth cannot be spent, it brings with it the violent compulsion to hoard. Go return it to the ghost this very minute and you will be a happy man again."

CHAPTER SEVENTY-EIGHT

THE INEVITABLE

A grieving mother approached Buddha, carrying the body of her dead child in her arms. She begged him, "I know you can bring him back to life." Buddha replied, "Death is inevitable; I cannot restore his life."

The woman was devastated, and was not prepared to accept this answer. Seeing her pain, Buddha said, "I can bring your child back to life, but only if you bring me mustard seeds from a person who has never had a death in his family."

Hearing these words, a new hope was awakened within the grieving mother's heart. Immediately she rushed out to beg for mustard seeds. She knocked at the first door and asked for some mustard seeds. The middle-aged lady answering the door was very kind and asked her to wait a moment. The woman asked, "There has not been a death in your family, has there?" The lady started crying and said, "Six months ago my husband died in his sleep." The mother was disappointed and she moved on.

The second person she approached was a young man, who said that his grandfather had passed away only a few days earlier. The third was an old woman who's grown up son and daughter-in-law had been killed in an accident. One after the other, the woman found that someone or the other had died in every family.

By the time the woman returned to Buddha, she had made peace with her son's death. She had accepted the inevitable.

CHAPTER SEVENTY-NINE

THE TRIPLE FILTER TEST

In ancient Greece, Socrates was reputed to hold knowledge in high esteem. One day an acquaintance met the great philosopher and said, "Do you know what I just heard about your friend?"

"Hold on a minute," Socrates replied. "Before you talk to me about my friend, it might be good idea to take a moment and filter what you're going to say. That's why I call it the triple filter test. The first filter is Truth. Have you made absolutely sure that what you are about to tell me is true?"

"Well, no," the man said, "actually I just heard about it and..."

"All right," said Socrates. "So you don't really know if it's true or not. Now, let's try the second filter, the filter of Goodness. Is what you are about to tell me about my friend something good?"

"Umm, no, on the contrary..."

"So," Socrates continued, "you want to tell me something bad about my friend, but you're not certain it's true. You may still pass the test though, because there's one filter left — the filter of Usefulness. Is what you want to tell me about my friend going to be useful to me?"

No, not really.

"Well," concluded Socrates, "if what you want to tell me is neither true, nor good, nor even useful, why tell it to me at all?"

CHAPTER EIGHTY

RICH FOREVER

Lord Shiva appeared to one of his devotees in a dream.

The devotee was a humble villager, who was caught between a rock and a hard place – he was a spiritual seeker who also wanted to be very wealthy. So that night, Lord Shiva appeared to him in a dream and told him, "If you were to go at dusk tomorrow to the outskirts of the village, you will see a sanyasi seated under a tree. Ask him for the stone that will make you rich forever!"

The villager woke up, every aspect of the dream etched into his memory. He spent the day going about his chores impatiently, eager waiting for dusk. As the sun began its descent, he rushed out from the village.

On the outskirts of the village, a sanyasi having spent the entire day travelling around, settled down under a tree to rest for the night, so that he could rise early, meditate and continue his journey. He was surprised to see a villager rushing towards him with glowing eyes.

"Oh Swami! I am so glad to see you, please give me the stone that you carry for me."

"What stone?" asked the sanyasi.

"Lord Shiva appeared in my dream last night and told me that you would give me a stone."

The sanyasi rummaged in his sack, and pulling out a stone, he said, "The Lord probably meant this one. I found it in the forest yesterday. Here, take it if you want it."

The villager gazed at the stone in awe and wonder. It was one of the largest diamonds in the world – almost as big as a fist. It would make him rich beyond imagination. He took it back with him, hid it in his house and went off to sleep.

But sleep was elusive, he tossed and turned as a hundred thoughts ran through his head. Eager to catch hold of the sanyasi before he left, he rushed out of the village before dawn to catch him meditating under the tree. He waited patiently for a while and when the sanyasi opened his eyes, he said, "Give me the wealth that makes it possible for you to give this tone away."

CHAPTER EIGHTY-ONE

TRY

A Guru advised his students to meditate three times each day. Most of his students listened to him attentively but with some trepidation.

Not one of this students said a simple 'yes'; most of them responded with 'I will try'.

The Guru nodded wisely and as he walked back to his seat, he 'accidentally' dropped the book he held under his arm and it fell to the floor. He turned back, bent over and reached for the book, but could not get it.

Stooping down several times in a row, he endeavoured to pick up his book but apparently failed on each occasion to grab it. His students looked at him stupefied.

"You try to pick it up." He told one of the students.

The student walked up to the book, bent over, picked it up in one quick motion and handed it to the Guru. The Guru knocked the book out of his hands and admonished him, "I did not ask you to pick up the book; I only asked you to try."

CHAPTER EIGHTY-TWO

THE GOLD RING

The young man was climbing the hill slowly, one step at a time. His bowed head seemed to indicate that something was bothering him. Perhaps he was lonely, or discouraged. He was coming to seek guidance from the wise man that lived on the hill on the outskirts of town.

Entering the counsellor's house, the young man found him reading, deep in thought.

"Excuse me, sir," he said hesitantly. The old man lifted his eyes. Timidly, with a courteous bow and a voice of desperation, the young man said, "I have come seeing your help, sir." After a short pause, he continued, "I have dreams that I believe I can achieve, but no one thinks I have the ability to reach them. People see little value in me."

The old man continued his reading. After a while, he said, "Before I can give you any counsel, I need your help. Are you willing?" Somewhat disappointed for having his own needs ignored, the young man nevertheless responded, "I will do my best, sir."

The wise man stood up. Stretching himself a bit, he said, "I may need to repay a large debt in the future, for which I will need money. Here is my gold ring. Take it to the market and find out how much I can get for it, but don't settle for anything less than five gold coins. There is my horse. Go!"

The young man held onto the ring tightly and upon reaching the market place, went from stall to stall, offering it in exchange for cash. The fruit seller ignored him. The clothes merchant told him that he was not interested. The farmer selling chickens continued to bargain with a customer and waved him away.

Finally, the young man reached the pig seller's stall. After examining the ring for a while in his dirty hand, he said with a covetous smirk, "Tell the owner that I man be willing to give him five bronze coins for this."

"I fulfilled your assignment, sir," said the young man upon his return. "No one in the market is willing to give five gold coins for your beautiful ring."

"That's fine," responded the wise man. Now we know how little the market people value this ring. Go to the jeweller in town and show it to him."

When the jeweller saw the gold ring, he quickly stood up and used a silk handkerchief to hold it carefully. Bring it under a lamp, he examined it in detail with a magnifying glass. "A masterpiece," he said softly. "If the owner if the ring is in hurry, I will buy it for 10 gold coins myself. But if he gives me time to bring out all its beauty, I shall find a wealthy customer willing to pay at least 20 gold coins for it."

The wise man listened attentively to the report the happy young man brought back and then told him, "Don't let the ignorant tell you the value of something they know nothing about. Listen only to the appraisal of the skilled specialist, the one who can recognize the true value of a master artist's work."

And with a smile, the wise man placed the golden ring back on his finger and waved the young man good-bye.

CHAPTER EIGHTY-THREE

THE WHITE ELEPHANT

Once upon a time, there lived a herd of eighty thousand elephants at the bottom of the majestic Himalayas. Their leader was a magnificent and rare white elephant who was an extremely kind-hearten soul. He greatly loved his mother who had grown blind and feeble and could not look out for herself.

Each day this white elephant would go deep into the forest in search of food. He would look for the best of wild fruit, especially jackfruit, to send to his mother. But alas, his mother never received any. This was because his messengers would always eat them up themselves. Each night, when he returned home he would be surprised to hear that his mother had been starving all day. He was absolutely disgusted with his herd.

Then one day, he decided to leave them all behind and disappeared in the middle of the night along with his dear mother. He took her to Mount Kabala to live in a cave beside a beautiful lake that was covered by gorgeous pink lotuses.

It so happened that one day, when the white elephant was feeding he heard loud cries. A forester from Benaras had lost his way in the forest and was absolutely terrified. He had come to the area to visit relatives and could not find his way out.

On seeing this big white elephant he was even more terrified and ran as fast as he could. The elephant followed him and told him not to be afraid, as all he wanted to do was to help him. He asked the forester why he was crying so bitterly. The forester replied that he was crying because he had been roaming the forest for the past seven days and could not find his way out.

The elephant told him not to worry as he knew every inch of this forest and could take him to safety. He then lifted him on to his back and carried him to the edge of the forest from where the forester went on his merry way back to Benaras.

On reaching the city, he heard that King Brahmadutta's personal elephant had just died and the King was looking for a new elephant. His heralds were roaming the city, announcing that any man who had seen or heard of an elephant fit for a King should come forward with the information.

The forester was very excited and immediately went up to the King and told him about the white elephant that he had seen on Mount Kabala. He told him that he had marked the way and would require the help of the elephant trainers in order to catch this fantastic elephant.

The King was quite pleased with the information and immediately dispatched a number of soldiers and elephant trainers along with the forester. After travelling for many days, the group reached the lake besides which the elephants resided. They slowly moved down to the edge of the lake and hid behind the bushes. The white elephant was collecting lotus shoots for his mother's meal and could sense the presence of humans. When he looked up, he spotted the forester and realized that it was he who had led the King's men to him. He was very upset at the ingratitude but decided that if he put up a struggle many of the men would be killed. And he was just too kind to hurt anyone. So he decided to go along with them to Benaras and then request the benevolent King to be set free.

That night when the white elephant did not return home, his mother was very worried. She had heard all the commotion outside and had guessed that the King's men had taken away her son. She was scared that the King would ride him in to battle and her son would definitely be killed. She was also worried that there would be no one to look after her or even feed her, as she could not see. She just lay down and cried bitterly.

Meanwhile her son was led in to the beautiful city of Benaras where he was given a grand reception. The whole city was decorated and his own stable was gaily painted and covered with garlands of fragrant flowers. The trainers laid out a feast for their new state elephant who refused to touch a morsel. He did not respond to any kind of stimuli, be it the fragrant flowers or the beautiful and comfortable stable. He just sat there looking completely despondent.

The worried trainers went straight to report the situation to their King, as they were scared that the elephant would just waste away without any food or water. The King was extremely concerned when he heard what they had to say and went to the stable himself. He offered the elephant food from the royal table and asked him why he grieved in this manner. He thought that the elephant should be proud and honoured that he was chosen as the state elephant and would get the opportunity to serve his King.

But the white elephant replied that he would not eat a thing until he met his mother. So the King asked him where his mother was. The elephant replied that she was back home on Mount Kabala and must be worried and hungry as she was blind and had no one to feed her and take care of her. He was afraid that she would die.

The compassionate King was touched by the elephant's story and asked him to return to his blind, old mother and take care of her as he had been doing all along. He set him free in love and kindness. The happy elephant went running home as fast as he could. And he was relieved to find that his mother was still alive. He filled his trunk with water and poured it over his sick mother who thought that it was raining. Then she cried out as she thought that some evil spirit had come to harm her and wished and prayed that her son was there to save her.

The white elephant gently bent over his blind mother and stroked her lovingly. She immediately recognized his touch and was overjoyed. Her son lifted her up and told her that the kind and compassionate King of Benaras had set him free and he was here to love and look after his mother forever.

His mother was absolutely thrilled and blessed the kind King with peace, prosperity and joy till the end of his days. She was so thankful to him for sending her son back home. The white elephant was able to take good care of his mother till the day she died. And when he died himself, the King erected a statue of him by the side of the lake and held an annual elephant festival there in memory of such a caring and noble soul.

CHAPTER EIGHTY-FOUR

THE THREE TREES

Once upon a time, there were three trees on a hill in the woods. They were discussing their hopes and dreams when the first tree said, "Someday I hope to be a treasure chest. I could be filled with gold, silver and precious gems. I could be decorated with intricate carving and everyone would see the beauty."

Then the second tree said, "Someday I will be a mighty ship. I will take Kings and queens across the waters and sail to the corners of the world. Everyone will feel safe in me because of the strength of my hull."

Finally the third tree said, "I want to grow to be the tallest and straightest Tree in the forest. People will see me on top of the hill and look up to my branches, and think of the heavens and God and how close to them I am reaching. I will be the greatest tree of all time and people will always remember me."

After a few years of praying that their dreams would come true, a group of woodsmen came upon the trees. When one came to the first tree he said, "This looks like a strong tree, I think I should be able to sell the wood to a carpenter," and he began cutting it down. The tree was happy, because he knew that the carpenter would make him into a treasure chest.

At the second tree the woodsman said, "This looks like a strong tree. I should be able to sell it to the shipyard." The second tree was happy because he knew he was on his way to becoming a mighty ship.

When the woodsmen came upon the third tree, the tree was frightened because he knew that if they cut him down his dreams would not come true. One of the woodsmen said, "I don't need anything special from my tree, I'll take this one," and he cut it down.

When the first tree arrived at the carpenters, he was made into a feed box for animals. He was then placed in a barn and filled with hay. This was not at all what he had prayed for. The second tree was cut and made into a small fishing boat. His dreams of being a mighty ship and carrying kings had come to an end. The third tree was cut into large pieces, and left alone in the dark.

The years went by, and the trees forgot about their dreams.

Then one day, a man and woman came to the barn. She gave birth and they placed the baby in the hay in the feed box that was made from the first tree. The man wished that he could have made a crib for the baby, but this manger would have to do. The tree could feel the importance of this event and knew that it had held the greatest treasure of all time.

Years later, a group of men got in the fishing boat made from the second tree. One of them was tired and went to sleep. While they were out on the water, a great storm arose and the tree didn't think it was strong enough to keep the men safe. The men woke the sleeping man, and He stood and said 'Peace' and the storm stopped. At this time, the tree knew that it had carried the King of Kings in its boat.

Finally, someone came and got the third tree. It was carried through the streets as the people mocked the man who was carrying it. When they came to a stop, the man was nailed to the tree and raised in the air to die at the top of a hill. When Sunday came, the tree came to realize that it was strong enough to stand at the top of the hill and be as close to God as was possible, because Jesus had been crucified on it.

The moral of this story is that when things don't seem to be going your way, always know that Creation has a plan for you.

Each of the trees got what they wanted, just not in the way they had imagined.

RUMOURS

Once an old man spread rumours that his neighbour was a thief. As a result, the young man was arrested. Days later the young man was proven innocent.

After being released he sued the old man for wrongly accusing him.

In the court, the old man told the Judge: "They were just comments, didn't harm anyone."

The judge told the old man: "Write all the things you said about him on a piece of paper. Cut them up and on the way home, throw the pieces of paper out. Tomorrow, come back to hear the sentence."

Next day, the judge told the old man: "Before the hearing starts, go out and gather all the pieces of paper that you threw out yesterday."

The old man said: "I can't do that! The wind spread them and I won't know where to find them."

The judge then replied: "The same way, simple comments may destroy the honour of a man to such an extent that one is not able to fix it. If you can't speak well of someone, rather don't say anything."

CHAPTER EIGHTY-SIX

TRUE GENEROSITY

Charkha, which was once the source of livelihood for artisans and the tool of choice for women, acquired a special significance during the freedom struggle when it became the symbol of Swadeshi movement which sought to bring about an economic revolution by discarding machine-made goods of the United Kingdom and replacing them with Indian hand-woven cloth. The emphasis on charkha had the twin objectives of alleviating poverty through supplementary income for villagers and impeding the flow of Indian money to the British industries.

Charkha was given a new meaning and novel interpretation by Mahatma Gandhi. Mahatma Gandhi went from city to city, village to village, collecting funds for the Charkha Sangh. During one of his tours, he addressed a meeting in Orissa. After he had completed his speech, a poor old grey-haired woman, bent with age, her clothes in tatters, fought her way to where Gandhiji was sitting, successfully thwarting the attempts of the volunteers to stop her from doing so.

"I must see him," she chanted, as she finally reached the platform, going up to Gandhiji and touching his feet. Then, from the folds of her sari, she brought out a copper coin and placed it at his feet. Gandhiji picked up the copper coin gently and put it away carefully.

The Charkha funds were then under the charge of Jamnalal Bajaj. He asked Gandhiji for the coin, but Gandhiji refused. "What's this?" queried Jamnalal Bajaj with a laugh, "I keep cheques and currency worth thousands of rupees for the Sangh and you will not trust me with a copper coin?"

Said Gandhiji, "This copper coin is worth much more than those thousands that you hold in your fund. If a man has several thousands and he gives away a hundred or two, it doesn't mean much. But this coin was probably all that the poor woman possessed. She gave me all that she had. That was very generous of her. What a great sacrifice she has made! That is why I value this coin much more than a lakh of rupees."

CHAPTER EIGHTY-SEVEN

THE ICE-CREAM ENGINEER

Purportedly a true story, Snopes (https://www.snopes.com/fact-check/cone-of-silence/) tags this as a 'legend'. *The Claim: A flavour of ice cream being transported affects a car's performance: every time vanilla is the driver's choice, the car stalls.*

A complaint was received by the Pontiac Division of General Motors: This is the second time I have written to you, and I don't blame you for not answering me, because I kind of sounded crazy, but it is a fact that we have a tradition in our family of ice cream for dessert after dinner each night. But the kind of ice cream varies so, every night, after we've eaten, the whole family votes on which kind of ice cream we should have and I drive down to the store to get it.

It's also a fact that I recently purchased a new Pontiac and since then my trips to the store have created a problem. You see, every time I buy vanilla ice cream, when I start back from the store my car won't start. If I get any other kind of ice cream, the car starts just fine.

I want you to know I'm serious about this question, no matter how silly it sounds: 'What is there about a Pontiac that makes it not start when I get vanilla ice cream, and easy to start whenever I get any other kind?'

The Pontiac President was understandably sceptical about the letter, but sent an engineer to check it out anyway. The latter was surprised to be greeted by a successful, obviously well-educated man in a fine neighbourhood. He had arranged to meet the man just after dinner time, so the two hopped into the car and drove to the ice cream store. It was vanilla ice cream that night and, sure enough, after they came back to the car, it wouldn't start.

The engineer returned for three more nights. The first night, the man got chocolate. The car started. The second night, he got strawberry. The car started. The third night he ordered vanilla. The car failed to start!

Now the engineer, being a logical man, refused to believe that this man's car was allergic to vanilla ice cream. He arranged, therefore, to continue his visits for as long as it took to solve the problem. And toward this end he began to take notes: he jotted down all sorts of data, time of day, type of gas used, time to drive back and forth, etc. In a short time, he had a clue: The man took less time to buy vanilla than any other flavour. Why? The answer was in the layout of the store.

Vanilla, being the most popular flavour, was in a separate case at the front of the store for quick pick-up. All the other flavours were kept in the back of the store at a different counter where it took considerably longer to find the flavour and get checked out. Now the question for the engineer was why the car wouldn't start when it took less time.

Once time became the problem — not the vanilla ice cream — the engineer quickly came up with the answer: *vapour lock*. It was happening every night, but the extra time taken to get the other flavours allowed the engine to cool down sufficiently to start. When the man got vanilla, the engine was still too hot for the vapour lock to dissipate.

Even insane-looking problems are sometimes real.

CHAPTER EIGHTY-EIGHT

WHEN YOUR HUT IS ON FIRE

The only survivor of a shipwreck was washed up on a small, uninhabited island.

He prayed feverishly for God to rescue him. Every day he scanned the horizon for help, but none seemed forthcoming. Exhausted, he eventually managed to build a little hut out of driftwood to protect him from the elements, and to store his few possessions.

One day, after scavenging for food, he arrived home to find his little hut in flames, with smoke rolling up to the sky. He felt the worst had happened, and everything was lost. He was stunned with disbelief, grief, and anger.

He cried out, "God! How could you do this to me?"

Early the next day, he was awakened by the sound of a ship approaching the island! It had come to rescue him!

"How did you know I was here?" asked the weary man of his rescuers. "We saw your smoke signal," they replied.

CHAPTER EIGHTY-NINE

THE MAGICAL BEGGING-BOWL

Whenever you desire something, your happiness depends on *that* something. If it is taken away, you are miserable; if it is given to you, you are happy. But only for the moment! That too has to be understood. Whenever your desire is fulfilled it is only for the moment that you feel happy. It is fleeting, because once you have got it, the mind starts desiring for more, for something else.

Mind exists by 'desiring'; hence the mind can never leave you without desire. If you are without desire, the mind collapses within itself. That's the whole secret of meditation.

A beggar knocks on the door of an emperor; it is early morning. The emperor was coming out for a morning walk in his beautiful garden; otherwise it would have been difficult for the beggar to have an appointment with him. But there was no mediator to prevent him.

The emperor said, "What do you want?"

The beggar said, "Before you ask that, think twice!"

The emperor has never seen such a lion of a man; he had fought wars, had won victories, had made it clear that nobody is more powerful than him, but suddenly this beggar had the audacity to tell him, 'Think twice about what you are committing yourself to, because you may not be able to fulfil it!'

The king (almost with a sneer) said, "Do not be worried, that is my concern; you ask what you want, it will be done!"

The beggar said, "You see my begging bowl? I want it to be filled! It does not matter what you fill it with, the only condition is that it should be filled, it should be full."

The emperor threw his head back and laughed, "Is that all? And you think I am not capable of this simple task?"

The beggar cautioned him once again, "Remember, you still have the option to refuse, but if you say yes, you are committed and you are then risking failure."

The emperor laughed. Just a beggar's bowl... and he is being given a warning? He told his premier to fill the beggar's bowl with diamonds, so that this audacious beggar would know who he was dealing with.

Quite soon it became apparent that the beggar was right, because the moment the diamonds were poured into his begging bowl they simply disappeared!

The word began to spread like wildfire in the capital; thousands of people arrived to watch. When the precious stones were finished the king said, "Bring out all the gold and silver, everything! My whole kingdom, my whole integrity is being challenged."

By evening, everything had disappeared and there were now two beggars - one of them used to be the emperor.

The emperor said, "Please forgive me for not heeding your warnings and treating you with contempt and condescension, do tell me the secret of this begging bowl."

The beggar said, "It is no secret. I have polished it, made it look like a bowl, but it is a human skull. Anything you pour into it, disappears."

This story is profound. Have you ever thought about your own begging bowl? Everything disappears - power, prestige, honour, stature, wealth; everything disappears and your begging bowl begs for more. The desire, the longing for something else takes you away from this moment.

There are only two kinds of people in the world: the majority are running after shadows; their begging bowls will remain with them till they enter their graves. And a very small minority, one in a million, stop running, drop all desires, ask for nothing, are content with what they have - and suddenly that one finds everything within oneself.

CHAPTER NINETY

THE APPLE TREE

A long time ago, there was a huge apple tree. A little boy loved to come and play around it every day. He climbed to the treetop, ate the apples, and took a nap under the shadow. He loved the tree and the tree loved to play with him.

Time went by, the little boy had grown up and he no longer played around the tree every day. One day, the boy came back to the tree and he looked sad.

"Come and play with me", the tree asked the boy.

"I am no longer a kid, I do not play around trees anymore" the boy replied, "I want toys. I need money to buy them."

"Sorry, but I do not have money, but you can pick all my apples and sell them. So, you will have money."

The boy was so excited. He grabbed all the apples on the tree and left happily. The boy never came back after he picked the apples. The tree was sad.

One day, the boy who now turned into a man returned and the tree was excited.

"Come and play with me" the tree said.

"I do not have time to play. I have to work for my family. We need a house for shelter. Can you help me?"

"Sorry, but I do not have any house. But you can chop off my branches to build your house." So the man cut all the branches of the tree and left happily.

The tree was glad to see him happy but the man never came back since then. The tree was once again lonely and sad.

One hot summer day, the man returned and the tree was delighted.

"Come and play with me!" the tree said.

"I am getting old. I want to go sailing to relax myself. Can you give me a boat?" asked the man.

"Use my trunk to build your boat. You can sail far away and be happy."

So the man cut the tree trunk to make a boat. He went sailing and never showed up for a long time. Finally, the man returned after many years.

"Sorry, my boy. But I do not have anything for you anymore. No more apples for you", the tree said.

"No problem, I do not have any teeth to bite" the man replied.

"No more trunk for you to climb on."

"I am too old for that now" the man said.

"I really cannot give you anything, the only thing left is my dying roots," the tree said with tears.

"I do not need much now, just a place to rest. I am tired after all these years," the man replied.

"Good! Old tree roots are the best place to lean on and rest, come sit down with me and rest." The man sat down and the tree was glad and shed tears of joy.

The apple tree in the story is synonymous with our parents and the manner in which many of us treat them.

We take what we want, and return when we need more or in times of trouble, since they are always there for us, showering unconditional love. We take them for granted; we do not appreciate all that they do for us, until it is way too late. We do not give them quality time or support; and think that an occasional phone call is all they need. Yes, they do not complain – just like the apple tree! We take it for granted!

If you think (after reading this story) that the boy was cruel to the apple tree.....

CHAPTER NINETY-ONE

NUTS AND BOLTS

A truck driver, who was carrying out his normal routine delivery at a mental asylum, parked his vehicle beside an open drain. He discovered the flat tyre, after completing his deliveries just as he was about to drive off. He jacked up the truck and unfastened the flat tyre in order to replace it with the spare tyre.

As luck would have it, when he was about to fix the spare tyre, he accidentally dropped all the four bolts into the open drain. Since he could not possibly fish out the bolts from the open drain, he began to panic. He got increasingly agitated as he realized there was practically nothing he could do to extricate the bolts from the drain.

Just then, one patient happened to walk past him and politely asked the driver, "Hey man, why are you looking so vexed and gloomy? What happened?"

The driver thought to himself - there is nothing much I can do or this mental joker can. But if I don't answer him, this nut is going to keep pestering me with questions.

So, in order to get rid of him quickly, the truck driver told him about whole episode and gave him a helpless look.

The patient just laughed at the truck driver and said, "Can you not fix such a simple problem? No wonder you are destined to remain a truck driver for life".

The truck driver was enraged and said with a sneer, "Oh – so you have an immediate solution to this problem, is it? Do let me know."

"Here is what you can do" said the patient, "take one bolt from each of the remaining 3 tyres / wheels and fix it on to this tyre. Then drive down to the nearest workshop and replace the missing ones. Isn't it simple, my friend?"

The truck driver stared at him amazed and surprised, "How come you are so smart and intelligent and you are here at the mental asylum?"

The patient replied "Hello friend! I stay here because I am crazy but not stupid".

CHAPTER NINETY-TWO

THE INTERVIEW

Appreciation is not the rewards & recognition program in corporate offices; appreciation is the empathy, the full understanding of a situation, the recognition of the effort that it takes to deliver results.

One young urban professional, an academically brilliant lad, applied for a senior managerial position in a large multinational.

He sailed through the series of interviews and assessments and was slotted to meet the Director, for the final interview and the outcome.

The Director gathered from the CV that the youth's academic achievements were excellent all the way from secondary school until the postgraduate research; never had there been a year when he did not score good grades.

The Director asked, "Did you obtain any scholarships in school?"

The youth answered "None."

"Was it your father who paid for your school fees?"

"My father passed away when I was a year old; it was my mother who paid for my school fees."

"Where did your mother work?"

"My mother worked as a clothes cleaner."

The Director requested the youth to show his hands. The youth showed a pair of hands that were smooth and perfect.

The Director asked, "Have you ever helped your mother wash the clothes before?"

"Never, my mother has always wanted me to study and read more books. Furthermore, my mother can wash clothes quicker and better than I ever could."

"I have a request. When you go back home today, go and clean your mother's hands, and then see me tomorrow morning."

The youth felt that his chance of landing the high-profile job was very high. When he went back, he happily requested his mother to let him clean her hands. His mother was surprised with this strange request, yet somehow happy and with mixed feelings, she showed her hands to the kid.

The youth cleaned his mother's hands slowly. For the first time, he wept.

It was the first time he noticed that his mother's hands were so wrinkled, and there were so many bruises in her hands. Some bruises were so painful that his mother grimaced and shivered as they were being cleaned.

The young lad realized that it was *this pair of hands* that washed the clothes every day to enable him to pay the school fee. The bruises in the mother's hands were the price that his mother had to pay for his graduation, academic excellence and his future.

Once he finished cleaning his mother's hands, the young lad, for the first time in his life, quietly washed all the residual clothes for his mother.

That night, mother and son talked for a very long time.

Next morning, the youth went to the Director's office.

The Director noticed the tears in the youth's eyes, asked, "Can you tell me about your experience and learning yesterday?"

The young lad answered, "I cleaned my mother's hand, and also finished cleaning all the remaining clothes."

The Director asked, "Please tell me the top three learnings."

The youth said, with all humility, "One. I know now the real meaning of appreciation. Without my mother, I would be nobody today. Likewise, without engaging with and appreciating my team members, I would be nobody in the organization."

"Two. By working together and helping my mother, I realize how difficult it is to get something done. Likewise, I should value the effort every peer and team member puts in an organization and work collaboratively."

"Three. I have come to appreciate the importance and value of family relationship. Likewise, building relationships in an organization is of vital importance."

The Director said, "This is what I am looking for to be my manager. I want to recruit a person who can appreciate the effort of other people and not take them for granted, a person who empathises and understands the difficulties that people face to get things done, and a person who would not put money as his only motivation and goal in life. You are hired!"

AFTERWORD: *A child, who has been protected and habitually given whatever he wanted, would develop "entitlement mentality" and would always put himself first. He would be ignorant of his parent's efforts. You can let your child live in a spacious house, eat well, learn the keyboard, watch a big screen TV. But when you are cutting grass or vegetables* or cooking and cleaning, please let them experience it. After a meal, encourage them to put away or wash their plates and bowls together with you. It is because you want to love them in a right way. You want them to empathize and understand, no matter how well-to-do their parents are. The most important thing your child should learn is how to appreciate the effort that everyone else puts in.

THE INVISIBLE ANGEL

The passengers on the bus watched sympathetically as the attractive young woman with the white cane made her way carefully up the steps. She paid the driver, using her hands to feel the location of the seats, walked down the aisle and found the seat he'd told her was empty. Then she settled in, placed her briefcase on her lap and rested her cane against her leg.

It had been a year since Susan, thirty-four, became blind. Due to a medical mis-diagnosis, she had been rendered sightless, and she was suddenly thrown into a world of darkness, anger, frustration and self-pity. Once a fiercely independent woman, Susan now felt condemned by this terrible twist of fate to become a powerless and helpless burden on everyone around her.

"How could this have happened to me?" she would plead, her heart knotted with anger, but no matter how much she cried, protested, ranted or prayed, she knew the painful truth that her sight was never going to return.

A cloud of depression hung over Susan's once optimistic spirit. Just getting through each day was an exercise in frustration and exhaustion. And all she had to cling to was her husband Mark.

Mark was an Air Force officer and he loved Susan unconditionally. When she first lost her sight, he watched her sink into despair and was determined to help his wife gain the strength and confidence she needed to become independent again.

Mark's military background had trained him well to deal with such sensitive situations, and yet he knew this was the most difficult battle he would ever face.

Finally, Susan felt ready to return to her job, but how would she get there? She used to take the bus, but was now too frightened to get around the city by herself. Mark volunteered to drive her to and from work each day, even though they worked at opposite ends of the city.

At first, this comforted Susan and fulfilled Mark's need to protect his sightless wife who was so insecure about performing the slightest task. Soon, however, Mark realized that this arrangement wasn't working, it was hectic and costly.

"Susan is going to have to start taking the bus again" he admitted to himself, but just the thought of mentioning it to her made him cringe, she was still so fragile and so angry. How would she react? He wondered.

Just as Mark predicted, Susan was horrified at the idea of taking the bus again. "I'm blind!" she responded bitterly "How am I supposed to know where I'm going? I feel like you're abandoning me."

Mark's heart shuddered to hear such words, but he knew what had to be done. He promised Susan that each morning and evening he would ride the bus with her, for as long as it took, until she got the hang of it. And that is exactly what happened.

For two solid weeks, Mark, military uniform and all, accompanied Susan to and from work each day. He taught her how to rely on her other senses specifically her hearing, how to determine where she was and how to adapt to her new environment. He helped her befriend the bus drivers who could watch out for her, and save her a seat. He made her laugh, even on those not-so-good days when she would trip exiting the bus, or drop her briefcase. Each morning they made the journey together, and Mark would take a cab back to his office.

Although this routine was even more costly and exhausting than the previous one, Mark knew it was only a matter of time before Susan would be able to ride the bus on her own. He believed in her, he used to know before she'd lost her sight, who wasn't afraid of any challenge and who would never, ever quit.

Finally, Susan decided that she was ready to try the trip on her own. Monday morning arrived, and before she left, she threw her arms around Mark, her temporary bus riding companion, her husband and her best friend. Her eyes filled with tears of gratitude for his loyalty, his sincerity, his patience and his love. She said good-bye, and for the first time, they went their separate ways. Monday, Tuesday, Wednesday, Thursday, each day on her own went perfectly, and Susan had never felt better. She was doing it and she was going to work all by herself.

On Friday morning, Susan took the bus to work as usual. As she was paying for her fare to exit the bus, the driver said "Boy, I sure envy you" Susan wasn't sure if the driver was speaking to her or not. After all, who on earth would ever envy a blind woman who had struggled just to find the courage to live for the past year?

Curiously, she asked him "Why do you say that you envy me?" The driver responded "It must feel so good to be taken care of and protected like you are". Susan had no idea what the driver was talking about, she asked him again "What do you mean?"

The driver answered, "You know, every morning for the past week, a fine looking gentleman in a military uniform has been standing across the corner watching you when you get off the bus. He makes sure you cross the street safely and he watches you until you enter your office building. Then he blows you a kiss, gives you a little salute and walks away. You are one lucky lady."

Tears of happiness poured down Susan's cheeks. For although she couldn't physically see him, she had always felt Mark's presence. She was fortunate, so fortunate, for he had given her a gift more powerful than sight, a gift she didn't need to see to believe, the gift of love that can bring light where there had been darkness. You don't love a woman because she is beautiful, but she is beautiful because you love her. It takes time for a woman to realize that!

CHAPTER NINETY-FOUR

SANDALWOOD

A poor old man lived in a forest and eked out his living by making charcoal from scraps of wood and selling it. One time, as a reward for rescuing a king who had lost his way in the forest, the poor man was given a beautiful grove full of most fragrant type of sandalwood trees. These trees were of a special quality from which expensive and rare perfume was made. One of these trees, in its natural state and without any effort on the part of the old man, was alone was worth more than the poor man could have earned during the rest of his life by producing and selling wood as charcoal.

Of course, the poor old man was very happy over this gift, but did not realize what a great fortune was bestowed on him. So, in order to make a living, he resorted to making charcoal out of sandalwood trees and selling it in the market for a pittance.

After a long time the king happened to pass that way again and noticed that the most valuable grove had been reduced to ashes, also that the old man was in the same poor condition as before. When the king enquired as to what had happened, the old man related that he had been earning his living by making charcoal from the trees.

The king then asked him if he had any sandalwood left. The old man replied that he had nothing except a small piece, perhaps, one or two feet long. The king told him to go to the same bazaar where he had been selling the charcoal and sell this piece of wood without first turning it into charcoal.

There were some wealthy people in the bazaar who noticed the excellent quality and rare fragrance of this piece of sandalwood. Recognizing its value, they all wanted to buy it. The result was that the old man earned hundreds of rupees out of that small one piece of sandalwood.

He returned to the king with the money, and the king said, "You have not appreciated the value of this wood. Had you appreciated it, you could have earned millions instead of paltry sum you did by selling it as charcoal and that too after going through the unnecessary labour of first making charcoal out of it."

On realizing his mistake, the old man asked the king for another such gift that he might make proper use of it. The king replied that such a gift is bestowed only once in a lifetime.

The human body, is the sandalwood, whose true value is realized only at the time of death, where man realizes he has squandered away his most precious possession and wishes he had realized its true value earlier.

CHAPTER NINETY-FIVE

BE THERE!

A nurse took the tired, anxious serviceman to the bedside. "Your son is here," she said to the old man. She had to repeat the words several times before the patient's eyes opened.

Heavily sedated because of the pain of his heart attack, he dimly saw the young uniformed Marine standing outside the oxygen tent. He reached out his hand. The Marine wrapped his toughened fingers around the old man's limp ones, squeezing a message of love and encouragement.

The nurse brought a chair so that the Marine could sit beside the bed. All through the night the young Marine sat there in the poorly lit ward, holding the old man's hand and offering him words of love and strength. Occasionally, the nurse suggested that the Marine move away and rest awhile.

He refused. Whenever the nurse came into the ward, the Marine was oblivious of her and of the night noises of the hospital - the clanking of the oxygen tank, the laughter of the night staff members exchanging greetings, the cries and moans of the other patients.

Now and then she heard him say a few gentle words. The dying man said nothing, only held tightly to his son all through the night.

Along towards dawn, the old man died. The Marine released the now lifeless hand he had been holding and went to tell the nurse. While she did what she had to do, he waited.

Finally, she returned. She started to offer words of sympathy, but the Marine interrupted her.

"Who was that man?" he asked.

The nurse was startled, "He was your father," she answered.

"No, he wasn't," the Marine replied. "I have never seen him in my life."

"Then why didn't you say something when I took you to him?"

"I knew right away there had been a mistake, but I also knew he needed his son, and his son just wasn't here. When I realized that he was too sick to tell whether or not I was his son, knowing how much he needed me, I stayed."

He continued, "I came here tonight to find a Mr. William Grey. His son was killed in Iraq today, and I was sent to inform him. What was this Gentleman's Name?"

The Nurse with tears in her eyes responded, "Mr. William Grey."

Forget the false courtesies that you often extend every day to say 'Hello' and talk about inconsequential irrelevant things. Instead, the next time someone needs you, just be there. We aren't human beings going through a temporary spiritual experience. We are spiritual beings going through a temporary human experience.

SYNERGIZE

By good fortune, Jack was able to raft down the Motu River in New Zealand twice during the previous year. The magnificent four-day journey traversed one of the last wilderness areas in North Island.

The first expedition was led by 'Buzz', an American guide with a great deal of rafting experience and many stories to tell of mighty rivers such as the Colorado. With a leader like Buzz, there was no reason to fear any of the great rapids on the Motu.

The first half day, in the gentle upper reaches, was spent developing teamwork and co-ordination. Strokes had to be mastered, and the discipline of following commands without question was essential. In the boiling fury of a rapid, there would be no room for any mistake. When Buzz bellowed above the roar of the water, an instant reaction was essential.

We mastered the Motu. In every rapid we fought against the river and we overcame it. The screamed commands of Buzz were matched only by the fury of our paddles, as we took the raft exactly where Buzz wanted it to go.

At the end of the journey, there was a great feeling of triumph. We had won. We proved that we were superior. We knew that we could do it. We felt powerful and good. The mystery and majesty of the Motu had been overcome.

The second time I went down the Motu, the experience I had gained should have been invaluable, but the guide on this journey was a very softly spoken Kiwi. It seemed that it would not even be possible to hear his voice above the noise of the rapids.

As we approached the first rapid, he never even raised his voice. He did not attempt to take command of us or the river. Gently and quietly he felt the mood of the river and watched every little whirlpool. There was no drama and no shouting. There was no contest to be won. He loved the river.

We sped through each rapid with grace and beauty and, after a day, the river had become our friend, not our enemy. The quiet Kiwi was not our leader, but only the person whose sensitivity was more developed than our own. Laughter replaced the tension of achievement.

Soon the quiet Kiwi was able to lean back and let all of us take turns as a leader. A quiet nod was enough to draw attention to the things our lack of experience prevented us from seeing. If we made a mistake, then we laughed and it was the next person's turn.

We began to penetrate the mystery of the Motu. Now, like the quiet Kiwi, we listened to the river and we looked carefully for all those things we had not even noticed the first time.

At the end of the journey, we had overcome nothing except ourselves. We did not want to leave behind our friend, the river. There was no contest, and so nothing had been won. Rather we had become *one with the river*.

It remains difficult to believe that the external circumstances of the two journeys were similar. The difference was in an attitude and a frame of mind. At the end of the journey, it seemed that there could be no other way.

CHAPTER NINETY-SEVEN

SITUATIONAL LEADERSHIP

Many years ago in a small Indian village, a farmer had the misfortune of owing a large sum of money to a village moneylender. The Moneylender, who was old and ugly, fancied the farmer's beautiful daughter. So he proposed a bargain.

He said he would forego the farmer's debt if he could marry his daughter. Both the farmer and his daughter were horrified by the proposal. So the cunning money-lender suggested that they let providence decide the matter. He told them that he would put a black pebble and a white pebble into an empty money bag. Then the girl would have to pick one pebble from the bag.

101.   If she picked the black pebble, she would become his wife and her father's debt would be forgiven.
102.   If she picked the white pebble, she need not marry him and her father's debt would still be forgiven.
103.   But if she refused to pick a pebble, her father would be thrown into Jail.

They were standing on a pebble strewn path in the farmer's field. As they talked, the moneylender bent over to pick up two pebbles. As he picked them up, the sharp-eyed girl noticed that he had picked up two black pebbles and put them into the bag.

The girl put her hand into the money bag and drew out a pebble. Without looking at it, she fumbled and let it fall onto the pebble-strewn path where it immediately became lost among all the other pebbles.

"Oh, how clumsy of me," she said. "But never mind, if you look into the bag for the one that is left, you will be able to tell which pebble I picked."

Since the remaining pebble is black, it must be assumed that she had picked the white one. And since the money-lender dared not admit his dishonesty, the girl changed what seemed an impossible situation into an extremely advantageous one.

CHAPTER NINETY-EIGHT

THE BRONZE RAT

A tourist walks into a curio shop in Colaba. Looking around at the exotic stuff on display, he notices a very lifelike, life-sized bronze statue of a rat. It has no price tag, but is so striking he decides he must have it.

He takes it to the owner, "How much for the bronze rat?"

"One hundred rupees for the rat, two thousand rupees for the story," says the owner.

The tourist gives the man a hundred bucks. "I'll just take the rat, you can keep the story."

As he walked down the street carrying his bronze rat, he noticed that a few real rats crawled out of the alleys and sewers and began following him down the street. This was vexing; he began to walk faster. But within a couple of blocks, the herd of rats behind him had grown to hundreds, and they began squealing in unison. He began to trot towards the Gateway of India, looking around to see that the rats now numbered in several thousands, and were still squealing and coming toward him rapidly.

Concerned, even scared, he runs to the edge of the wall opposite the Taj and throws the bronze rat as far out into the bay as he can. Amazingly, the millions of rats all jump into the bay after it, and are all drowned.

The man walked back to the curio shop.

"Aha," says the owner, "You have come back for the story?"

"No," said the man, "I came back to see if you have a statue of a politician in bronze!"

CHAPTER NINETY-NINE

THE FOX AND THE LION

'What an astonishing sight!' cried a Monk, having come across a fox that had no feet or legs, in a desolate forest.

'How can it possibly live?' he wondered, 'for it looks healthy enough.'

Then he jumped behind a rock in terror. A lion had come upon the scene.

The lion had killed a jackal. It dropped the carcass near the fox, ate its fill, and then went off, leaving bits of the meat behind. Quickly the fox ate the lot.

'Even more astonishing!' gasped the Monk. He couldn't believe what he had seen so next day he came out into the desert and again hid behind the rock. The same thing happened. The lion appeared with a freshly killed jackal, ate what it wanted, leaving portions of the meat for the fox to finish.

'It's a sign from God!' the Monk said to himself. 'From now on I, too, will rely, like the fox, upon the generosity of the Creator. He found himself a dark corner against a wall and settled to wait.

'God will provide,' he said to himself.

He sat there for several days and neither friend nor stranger went near him. More days passed. He grew thinner and thinner until his veins and skin were stretched like harp strings on his bony frame.

At length, when he was almost too weak to move, a holy man stood before him and enquired what the matter was.

The Monk poured out his story. "Now tell me," he said when he had finished, "Surely that was a sin from God?"

"Of course it was," replied the holy man, "but how could you be such an idiot? Why didn't you see that you were supposed to imitate, not the fox but the lion?"

ROSE

The first day of school our professor introduced himself and challenged us to get to know someone we didn't already know.

I stood up to look around when a gentle hand touched my shoulder. I turned around to find a wrinkled, little old lady beaming up at me with a smile that lit up her entire being.

She said, "Hi handsome. My name is Rose. I'm eighty-seven years old. Can I give you a hug?"

I laughed and enthusiastically responded, "Of course you may!" and she gave me a loving squeeze.

"Why are you in college at such a young, innocent age?" I asked.

She jokingly replied, "I'm here to meet a rich husband, get married, and have a couple of kids."

"No, seriously," I asked. I was curious what may have motivated her to be taking on this challenge at her age.

"I always dreamed of having a college education and now I'm getting one!" she told me.

After class we walked to the student union building and shared a chocolate milkshake. We became instant friends. Every day for the next three months, we would leave class together and talk nonstop. I was always mesmerized listening to this 'time machine' as she shared her wisdom and experience with me.

Over the course of the year, Rose became a campus icon and she easily made friends wherever she went. She loved to dress up and she revelled in the attention bestowed upon her from the other students. She was living it up.

At the end of the semester we invited Rose to speak at our football banquet. I'll never forget what she taught us. She was introduced and stepped up to the podium.

As she began to deliver her prepared speech, she dropped her three by five cards on the floor. Frustrated and a little embarrassed she leaned into the microphone and simply said, "I'm sorry I'm so jittery. I gave up beer for Lent and this whiskey is killing me! I'll never get my speech back in order so let me just tell you what I know."

As we laughed she cleared her throat and began, "We do not stop playing because we are old; we grow old because we stop playing. There are only four secrets to staying young, being happy, and achieving success. You have to laugh and find humour every day."

"You've got to have a dream. When you lose your dreams, you die. We have so many people walking around who are dead and don't even know it! There is a huge difference between growing older and growing up."

"If you are nineteen years old and lie in bed for one full year and don't do one productive thing, you will turn twenty years old. If I am eighty-seven years old and stay in bed for a year and never do anything I will turn eighty-eight."

"Anybody can grow older. That doesn't take any talent or ability. The idea is to grow up by always finding opportunity in change. Have no regrets."

"The elderly usually don't have regrets for what we did, but rather for things we did not do. The only people who fear death are those with regrets."

She concluded her speech by courageously singing 'The Rose'.

She challenged each of us to study the lyrics and live them out in our daily lives.

At the year's end Rose finished the college degree she had begun all those years ago. One week after graduation Rose died peacefully in her sleep.

Over two thousand college students attended her funeral in tribute to the wonderful woman who taught by example that it is never too late to be all you can possibly be. When you finish reading this, please send this peaceful word of advice to your friends and family, they'll really enjoy it!

Growing old is mandatory, Growing up is optional!

Stories have power. They delight, enchant, touch, teach, recall, inspire, motivate, challenge. They help us understand. They imprint a picture on our minds. Want to make a point or raise an issue? Tell a story.
– Janet Litherland

Do you have a story you would like to share?

Write in to me@rajeshseshadri.com or visit www.rajeshseshadri.com

With many thanks to all storytellers and
the three people who make my world go
around – my mother, my wife and my son.